John Clark Murray

Outline of Sir William Hamilton's Philosophy

A text-book for students

John Clark Murray

Outline of Sir William Hamilton's Philosophy
A text-book for students

ISBN/EAN: 9783337068424

Printed in Europe, USA, Canada, Australia, Japan

Cover: Foto ©Paul-Georg Meister /pixelio.de

More available books at **www.hansebooks.com**

OUTLINE

OF

SIR WILLIAM HAMILTON'S PHILOSOPHY.

A TEXT-BOOK FOR STUDENTS.

BY THE

REV. J. CLARK MURRAY,

PROFESSOR OF MENTAL AND MORAL PHILOSOPHY, QUEEN'S UNIVERSITY, CANADA.

With an Introduction,

BY THE

REV. JAMES McCOSH, LL.D,

PRESIDENT OF PRINCETON COLLEGE, NEW JERSEY.

BOSTON:
GOULD AND LINCOLN,
59 WASHINGTON STREET.
NEW YORK: SHELDON AND COMPANY.
CINCINNATI: G. S. BLANCHARD & CO.
TORONTO, ONT.: ADAM, STEVENSON & CO.
1871.

ROCKWELL & CHURCHILL, Printers, Boston.

To the Memory

OF

SIR WILLIAM HAMILTON,

THIS ESSAY

IN THE EXPOSITION OF HIS PHILOSOPHY

Is Inscribed

BY

A GRATEFUL PUPIL.

———◆———

"On Earth there is nothing great but Man:
In Man there is nothing great but Mind."

PREFACE.

—◦⟡◦—

THE primary object of this work is to provide a convenient text-book in philosophy. The labors of Sir William Hamilton as a professor formed generally the most powerful influence in the philosophical education of those who came within their reach; and a similar influence has extended into wider circles through his writings. It seemed to me, therefore, that his philosophy might still be made a valuable instrument of philosophical culture.

The chief difficulty in the way of this lay in the selection of one of his works, suitable for use as a text-book. A very slight acquaintance with these is sufficient to show that none of them by itself presents a complete view of his philosophical opinions in systematic order.[1] The *Lectures on Metaphysics*,

---

[1] For many readers it may not be unnecessary to enumerate the works of Sir William Hamilton. (1.) His edition of *Reid's Works* (1846) contains, besides many valuable footnotes, a number of supplementary dissertations on various philosophical subjects. Only a few of the intended dissertations were ever completed; but since his death his editors have published the fragmentary materials he had collected for the dissertations which had been left unfinished. (2.) The articles which he had contributed to the Edinburgh Review were collected into one volume, with numerous additions, under the title of *Discussions in Philosophy and Literature, Education and University Reform* (1852). (3.) The lectures, which he had been in the habit of delivering to his classes, were published posthumously; the *Lectures on Metaphysics*, in 1859; the *Lectures on Logic*, in 1860.

which contain the fullest account of his philosophy, and from which, therefore, the largest extracts have been drawn for the present work, besides being devoted mainly to one subdivision of his system, fail to give his matured views, or the matured expression of his views, on some subjects, while the discussion of many points is overladen with a mass of extraneous matter, which is generally confusing to the beginner and unnecessary for the comprehension of Hamilton's own system. I have, therefore, thought it advisable to attempt the systematic exhibition of his philosophical opinions without regard to the order or the mode of treatment which he has followed in any of his writings.

In doing so, however, it was necessary to adopt some order; and it seemed to me that I had no right to adopt any other than that which the philosopher has himself suggested in his distribution of the philosophical sciences,[1] though he has nowhere been able to carry it out. This distribution may possess comparatively little merit, and has certainly exerted no influence in directing the course of speculative thought in Europe or America, such as has flowed from Hegel's or from Comte's classification of the sciences; but the system of Hamilton would be inadequately represented by following any other course than that which I have adopted.

With regard to the liberties which I have taken in the composition of this *Outline*, I may remark, in the first place, that it has frequently been necessary to transfer passages from their original contexts, and that, in doing so, I have introduced them into their new contexts by such connecting particles and phrases as seemed most appropriate. I have

[1] See *Lectures on Metaphysics*, VII

also frequently left out of a passage a few words which were not essential to its meaning, especially when they appeared to be intended rather for an audience than for readers. Such slight liberties I have not considered it necessary to indicate. Occasionally, moreover, where Hamilton's editors intimate that he has adopted the language of another writer for the expression of his views, I have not preserved the marks of quotation, as these might have been confusing to a student. In one or two instances, however, I have ventured on an independent or abridged statement of Hamilton's doctrine; but such passages have been uniformly pointed out in the footnotes. It may also be added that I am responsible for the tabular classifications at pages 83 and 88, as well as for some slight alterations of expression in the others. With these explanations it may be said that the text is wholly Hamilton's.

As an exposition of Hamilton's Philosophy, the *Outline* contains some imperfections which were unavoidable. Even in the language these may at times be traced: for, while the volume is in the form of a text-book for private study, the largest portion of it is extracted from lectures which were intended to be delivered to a class; and though I have endeavored to leave out all the most obtrusive expressions of direct address, it was impossible to destroy the general form of phraseology. Some passages, moreover, undoubtedly suffer from being used as an exposition of a doctrine in a different connection and in a different point of view from that in which they were originally written. I believe, however, that no liberty which I have taken in the composition of the book has originated a single misrepresentation of Hamilton's opinions, while the whole volume offers a fair representation of his complete philosophical system. At the same time I do not take the responsibility of recommending that my book should be accepted as a final authority in any important question concerning Hamilton's doctrine, without referring to the works of the philosopher himself. I have, therefore, uniformly subjoined, within parentheses, a distinct reference to the place in his works from which each passage of the *Outline* is extracted; and, to prevent mistake, I may observe that each reference embraces the whole passage between it and the previous reference. I am not without hope, therefore, that, while the *Outline* may serve the purpose for which it is primarily designed, it may also be of some use to those who desire an acquaintance with Sir William Hamilton's system of philosophy, and have found the state of his writings a formidable obstacle in their way.

I have only to add that the work is merely expository, and that, therefore, while I have avoided any criticism of Hamilton's doctrines, I do not always undertake the responsibility of their defence. I believe, however, that the teaching of philosophy must still, at least, be conducted by helping the student to master the varying points of view from which the different representative systems look out on the field of speculation. For this reason, I trust that a slight service has been rendered to the cause of philosophical education by presenting, with a completeness which has never before been attempted, the system of Sir William Hamilton.

J. CLARK MURRAY.

QUEEN'S COLLEGE, ONT., October, 1870.

CONTENTS.

FIRST DIVISION OF PHILOSOPHY.

PHENOMENAL PSYCHOLOGY.

INTRODUCTION TO PHENOMENAL PSYCHOLOGY.

CHAPTER I.

DEFINITION OF THE SCIENCE, AND EXPLANATION OF TERMS IN THE DEFINITION.

CHAPTER II.

CONSCIOUSNESS IN GENERAL.

FIRST PART OF PHENOMENAL PSYCHOLOGY.

PHENOMENOLOGY OF THE COGNITIONS.

INTRODUCTION.

CLASSIFICATION OF THE COGNITIVE FACULTIES.

CHAPTER I.

THE PRESENTATIVE FACULTY.

CHAPTER II.

THE CONSERVATIVE FACULTY.

CHAPTER III.

THE REPRODUCTIVE FACULTY.

CHAPTER IV.

THE REPRESENTATIVE FACULTY.

CHAPTER V.

THE ELABORATIVE FACULTY.

CHAPTER VI.

THE REGULATIVE FACULTY.

APPENDIX TO CHAPTER VI.

LAW OF THE CONDITIONED IN ITS APPLICATION TO THE PRIN-
CIPLE OF CAUSALITY.

SECOND PART OF PHENOMENAL PSYCHOLOGY.

PHENOMENOLOGY OF THE FEELINGS.

INTRODUCTION.

CHAPTER I.

ABSTRACT THEORY OF PLEASURE AND PAIN.

CHAPTER II.

THE ABSTRACT THEORY APPLIED TO THE CONCRETE PHENOMENA.

THIRD PART OF PHENOMENAL PSYCHOLOGY.

PHENOMENOLOGY OF THE CONATIONS.

SECOND DIVISION OF PHILOSOPHY.

NOMOLOGICAL PSYCHOLOGY.

THIRD DIVISION OF PHILOSOPHY.

INFERENTIAL PSYCHOLOGY.

CHAPTER I.

EXISTENCE IN GENERAL.

CHAPTER II.

EXISTENCE OF GOD AND IMMORTALITY OF THE SOUL.

INTRODUCTORY NOTE.

Sir William Hamilton was the greatest metaphysician of his age, and his metaphysics will be studied by thinking minds in all coming ages. But his system was not drawn out in a compendious form by himself. In order to find it, students have to search a number of treatises in the shape of reviews, dissertations, class-lectures, notes, and notes upon notes. The stablished metaphysician delights in all this as an exhibition of the working of Hamilton's penetrating intellect, and because of the value of the seeds which, in the exuberance of his learning, he scatters in his progress. But as he often moves with great rapidity, and turns off at sharp angles into collateral discussions, the younger student is apt to be left behind and to become perplexed, and he longs to have some guide who may furnish him with a clear and combined view of the philosophy as a whole. This felt want has been supplied in Professor Murray's "Outline of Hamilton's Philosophy."

I have carefully read the work in proof, and I am able to say that it furnishes an admirable summary, — clear, correct, and readily intelligible, of the leading doctrines and connections of Hamilton's Philosophy. The account is rendered mainly in Hamilton's own language, by one who understands his philosophy, and who has the higher merit of entering thoroughly into the spirit of his great teacher. I have observed that in points in regard to which there have been disputes as to Hamilton's meaning, Professor Murray seems to me to give the proper version.

Those who are led by this brief exposition to take a general view, as from a height to which Professor Murray has conducted them, of the country spread out before them, will be allured, when he has left them, to enter upon a more particular exploration for themselves, when they will find innumerable scattered ore which could not have a place in a mere Outline.

The testimony now given will not be esteemed of less value because it comes from one who feels that Hamilton has often followed Kant's Critical Method too implicitly, and who dissents from his doctrines of Causality, of the Relativity of Knowledge, and of the negative nature of our Idea of the Infinite.

JAMES McCOSH.

PRINCETON, New Jersey, U. S., Oct. 1, 1870.

INTRODUCTION.

THE GENERAL NATURE AND DIVISIONS OF PHILOSOPHY.

---

§ 1. *THE GENERAL NATURE OF PHILOSOPHY.*

In commencing a course of philosophical discipline, it is important to obtain, at least, a general notion of what philosophy is. In order to this, there are two questions to be answered: (*A*) What is the meaning of the *name?* and (*B*) What is the meaning of the *thing?*

(*A*) *Nominal Definition of Philosophy.* Philosophy is a term of Greek origin, — it is a compound of φίλος, a *lover* or *friend*, and σοφία, *wisdom* — speculative wisdom. Philosophy is thus, literally, *a love of wisdom.* But if the grammatical meaning of the word be unambiguous, the history of its application is involved in considerable doubt. According to the commonly received account, the designation of philosopher was first assumed and applied by Pythagoras; but this rests on very slender authority. It is probable, I think, that Socrates was the first who adopted, or, at least, the first who familiarized, the

19

expression. It was natural that he should be anxious to contradistinguish himself from the Sophists (οἱ σοφοί, οἱ σοφισταί), literally, the *wise* men ; and no term could more appropriately ridicule the arrogance of these pretenders, or afford a happier contrast to their haughty designation, than that of philosopher (*i. e.*, the *lover* of wisdom) ; and at the same time it is certain that the substantives φιλοσοφία and φιλόσοφος first appear in the writings of the Socratic school. It is true, indeed, that the verb φιλοσοφεῖν is found in Herodotus (I. 30) ; and that, too, in a participial form, to designate a man who had travelled abroad for the purpose of acquiring knowledge. It is, therefore, not impossible that, before the time of Socrates, those who devoted themselves to the pursuit of the higher branches of knowledge were occasionally designated philosophers ; but it is far more probable that Socrates and his school first appropriated the term as a distinctive appellation ; and that the word *philosophy*, in consequence of this appropriation, came to be employed for the complement of all higher knowledge, and more especially to denote the science conversant about the principles or causes of existence.

(*B*) *Real Definition of Philosophy.* It is, perhaps, impossible adequately to define philosophy. For what is to be defined comprises what cannot be included in a single definition. For philosophy is not regarded from a single point of view ; it is sometimes considered as theoretical, that is, in relation to man as a thinking and cognitive intelligence ; sometimes as practical, that is, in relation to man as a moral agent; and sometimes as comprehending both theory and practice. Again, philosophy may either be regarded objectively, that is, as a complement of truth known; or subjectively, that is, as a habit or quality of the mind knowing. In these circumstances I shall not attempt a definition of philosophy, but shall endeavor to accomplish the end which every definition proposes, — make you understand, as precisely as the unprecise nature of the object-matter permits, what is meant by philosophy, and what are the sciences it properly comprehends within its sphere.

All philosophy is knowledge, but all knowledge is not philosophy. Philosophy is, therefore, a kind of knowledge. What, then, is philosophical knowledge, and how is it discriminated from knowledge in general?

I. We are endowed by our Creator with certain faculties of observation, which enable us to become aware of certain appearances or phenomena. These faculties may be stated as two, — Sense or External Perception, and Self-Consciousness or Internal Perception; and these faculties severally afford us the knowledge of a different series of phenomena. (1.) Through our senses we apprehend what exists or what occurs in the external or material world; (2.) By our self-consciousness, what is or what occurs in the internal world or world of thought. The information which we thus receive is called Historical or Empirical knowledge.

1. It is called *historical*, because, in this knowledge, we know only the fact, only that the phenome-

non is ; for history is properly only the narration of a consecutive series of phenomena in time, or the description of a coexistent series of phenomena in space. Civil history is an example of the one; natural history, of the other.

, 2. It is called *empirical* or *experiential*, if we might use that term, because it is given us by experience or observation, and not obtained as the result of inference or reasoning.

Historical or empirical knowledge is, therefore, simply the knowledge that something is. Were we to use the expression, *the knowledge that*, it would sound awkward and unusual in our modern languages. In Greek, the most philosophical of all tongues, its parallel, however, was familiarly employed. It was called τὸ ὅτι, that is, ἡ γνῶσις ὅτι ἔστιν. I should notice, that with us *the knowledge that*, is commonly called the knowledge of the *fact*. As examples of empirical knowledge, take the facts, whether known in our own experience or on the testified experience of others, that a stone falls, — that smoke ascends, — that the leaves bud in spring, and fall in autumn, — that such a book contains such a passage, — that such a passage contains such an opinion, — that Cæsar, that Charlemagne, that Napoleon existed.

II. But things do not exist, events do not occur, isolated — apart — by themselves ; they occur, and are conceived by us, only in connection. Our observation affords us no example of a phenomenon which is not an effect ; nay, our thought cannot even realize to itself the possibility of a phenomenon without a cause. We do not at present inquire into the nature of the connection of effect and cause, either in reality or in thought. It is sufficient for our present purpose to observe that, while, by the constitution of our nature, we are unable to conceive anything to begin to be without referring it to some cause, — still the knowledge of its particular cause is not involved in the knowledge of any particular effect. By this necessity, which we are under, of thinking some cause for every phenomenon; and by our original ignorance of what particular causes belong to what particular effects, — it is rendered impossible for us to acquiesce in the mere knowledge of the fact of a phenomenon; on the contrary, we are determined, we are necessitated, to regard each phenomenon as only partially known, until we discover the causes on which it depends for its existence. For example, we are struck with the appearance in the heavens called a rainbow. Think we cannot that this phenomenon has no cause, though we may be wholly ignorant of what that cause is. Now, our knowledge of the phenomenon as a mere fact — as a mere isolated event — does not content us; we therefore set about an inquiry into the cause, — which the constitution of our mind compels us to suppose, — and at length discover that the rainbow is the effect of the refraction of the solar rays by the watery particles of a cloud. Having ascertained the cause, but not till then, we are satisfied that we fully know the effect.

Now, this knowledge of the cause of a phenomenon is different from, is something more than, the knowledge of that phenomenon simply as a fact; and these two cognitions or knowledges have, accordingly, received different names. The latter, we have seen, is called historical or empirical knowledge; the former is called *philosophical* or *scientific* or *rational* knowledge. Historical, is the knowledge *that* a thing is; philosophical, the knowledge *why* or *how* it is. The Greek language well expresses philosophical knowledge as the διότι, — the γνῶσις διότι ἔστι.

Such is philosophical knowledge in its most extensive signification; and in this signification all the sciences occupied in the research of causes may be viewed as so many branches of philosophy. There is, however, one section of these sciences which is denominated philosophical by pre-eminence, — sciences which the term philosophy exclusively denotes, when employed in propriety and rigor. What these sciences are, and why the term philosophy has been specially limited to them, I shall now endeavor to make you understand.

"Man," says Protagoras, "is the measure of the universe:" and in so far as the universe is an object of knowledge, the paradox is a truth. Whatever we know, or endeavor to know, we know and can know only in so far as we possess a faculty of knowing in general; and we can only exercise that faculty under the laws which control and limit its operations. However great and infinite and various, therefore, may be the universe and its contents, these are known, not as they exist, but as our mind is capable of knowing them.

1. In the first place, therefore, as philosophy is a knowledge, and as all knowledge is only possible under the conditions to which our faculties are sub-

jected, the grand, the primary problem of philosophy must be to investigate and determine these conditions as the necessary conditions of its own possibility.

2. In the second place, as philosophy is not merely a knowledge, but a knowledge of causes, and as the mind itself is the universal and principal concurrent cause in every act of knowledge; philosophy is, consequently, bound to make the mind its first and paramount object of consideration. The study of mind is thus the philosophical study by pre-eminence. There is no branch of philosophy which does not suppose this as its preliminary, which does not borrow from this its light. In short, the science of mind, whether considered in itself or in relation to the other branches of knowledge, constitutes the principal and most important object of philosophy, — constitutes in propriety, with its suite of dependent sciences, philosophy itself.

From what has been said, you will, without a definition, be able to form at least a general notion of what is meant by philosophy. In its *more extensive signification*, it is equivalent to *a knowledge of things by their causes;* while, in its *stricter meaning*, it is confined to *the sciences which constitute, or hold immediately of, the science of mind.* (*Metaph., Lecture* III.)

§ 2. CLASSIFICATION OF THE PHILOSOPHICAL SCIENCES.

The whole of philosophy is an answer to three questions: (1.) What are the Facts or Phenomena to be observed? (2.) What are the Laws which regulate these facts, or under which these phenomena appear? (3.) What are the real Results, not immediately manifested, which these facts or phenomena warrant us in drawing?

I. If we consider the mind merely with the view of observing and generalizing the various phenomena it reveals, we have one mental science or one department of mental science; and this we may call the *Phenomenology of Mind.* It is commonly called *Psychology,* — *Empirical Psychology,* or the *Inductive Philosophy of Mind:* we might call it PHENOMENAL PSYCHOLOGY. It is evident that the divisions of this Science will be determined by the classes into which the phenomena of mind are distributed. I shall hereafter show you that there are three great classes of these phenomena, — namely, (1.) the phenomena of our Cognitive faculties, or faculties of Knowledge; (2.) the phenomena of our Feelings, or of Pleasure and Pain; (3.) the phenomena of our Conative powers, or of Will and Desire.

II. If, again, we analyze the mental phenomena with the view of discovering and considering, not contingent appearances, but the *necessary* and *universal* facts, that is, the Laws, by which our faculties are governed, to the end that we may obtain a criterion by which to judge or to explain their procedures and manifestations, we have a science which we may call the *Nomology of Mind,* or NOMOLOGICAL PSYCHOLOGY. Now, there will be as many distinct classes of Nomological Psychology as there are distinct classes of mental phenomena under the Phenomenological division.

III. The third great branch of philosophy is that which is engaged in the deduction of Inferences or Results. In the first branch philosophy is properly limited to the facts afforded in consciousness, considered exclusively in themselves. But these facts may be such as not only to be objects of knowledge in themselves, but likewise to furnish us with grounds of inference to something out of themselves. As effects, and effects of a certain character, they may enable us to infer the analogous character of their unknown causes; as phenomena, and phenomena of peculiar qualities, they may warrant us in drawing many conclusions regarding the distinctive character of that unknown substance, of which they are the manifestations. Now, the science conversant about all such inference of unknown being from its manifestations, is called *Ontology*, or *Metaphysics Proper*. We might call it INFERENTIAL PSYCHOLOGY.

The following is a tabular view of the distribution of philosophy as here proposed : —

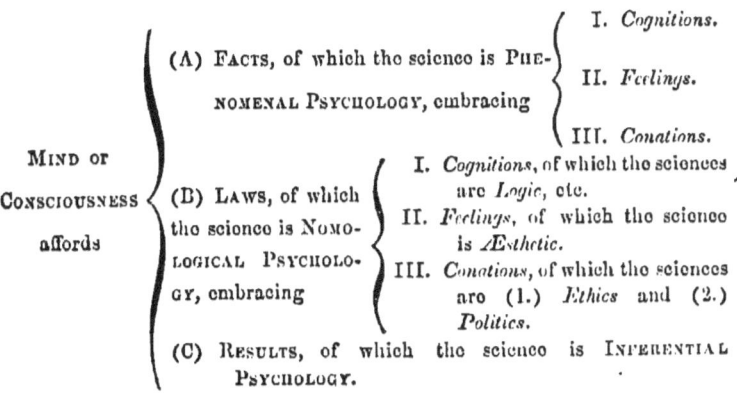

MIND or CONSCIOUSNESS affords

(A) FACTS, of which the science is PHENOMENAL PSYCHOLOGY, embracing
- I. *Cognitions.*
- II. *Feelings.*
- III. *Conations.*

(B) LAWS, of which the science is NOMOLOGICAL PSYCHOLOGY, embracing
- I. *Cognitions*, of which the sciences are *Logic*, etc.
- II. *Feelings*, of which the science is *Æsthetic*.
- III. *Conations*, of which the sciences are (1.) *Ethics* and (2.) *Politics*.

(C) RESULTS, of which the science is INFERENTIAL PSYCHOLOGY.

FIRST DIVISION OF PHILOSOPHY.

PHENOMENAL PSYCHOLOGY.

CHAPTER I.

DEFINITION OF THE SCIENCE AND EXPLANATION OF TERMS IN THE DEFINITION.

PHENOMENAL PSYCHOLOGY — Psychology, strictly so denominated — is the science conversant about the *phenomena or modifications or states of the Mind or Conscious Subject or Soul or Spirit or Self or Ego.*

In this definition I have purposely accumulated a variety of expressions, in order that I might have the earliest opportunity of making you accurately acquainted with their meaning. Before, therefore, proceeding further, I shall pause a moment in explanation of the terms in which this definition is expressed.

The term *Psychology* itself is a Greek compound, its elements being ψυχή, signifying *soul* or *mind*, and λόγος, signifying *discourse* or *doctrine*. Psychology is, therefore, the *discourse* or *doctrine treating of the human mind.*

The above definition of psychology contains two correlative sets of terms, — the one designating the phenomena of knowing, willing, feeling, desiring, etc.,

31

in which the mind becomes known; the other designating the mind, considered as the unknown substance to which these phenomena belong.   Of the
former class are the words *phenomenon, mode, modification, state;* and to these may be added the analogous
terms *quality, property, attribute, accident.*   Of the
latter class are *subject, mind, soul, spirit, self, ego.*

(*A*) Terms expressing the Manifestations of
the Mind.

I. *Phenomenon* is the Greek word for *that which
appears,* and may therefore be translated by *appearance.*
There is, however, a distinction to be noticed. (1.) In
the first place, the employment of a Greek term shows
that it is used in a strict and philosophical application. (2.) In the second place, the term *appearance* is
used to denote not only that which reveals itself to
our observation, as existent, but also that which only
seems to be, in contrast to that which truly is.   There
is thus not merely a certain vagueness in the word,
but it even involves a kind of contradiction to the
sense in which it is used when employed for *phenomenon.*   In consequence of this, the term phenomenon
has been naturalized in our language as a philosophical substitute for the term appearance.   The terms
phenomenon and appearance are employed in reference
to a substance, as known; the remaining terms, in
reference to a substance, as existing.

II. A *mode* is the manner of the existence of anything.   Take, for example, a piece of wax.   The wax
may be round, or square, or of any other definite figure; it may also be solid or fluid.   Its existence in
any of these modes is not essential; it may change

from one to the other without any substantial alteration. As the mode cannot exist without a substance, we can accord to it only a secondary or precarious existence in relation to the substance, to which we accord the privilege of existing by itself, *per se existere;* but though the substance be not restricted to any particular mode of existence, we must not suppose that it can exist, or at least be conceived by us to exist, in none. All modes are, therefore, variable states ; and though some mode is necessary for the existence of a thing, any individual mode is accidental.

III. *Modification* is properly the bringing a thing into a certain mode of existence ; but it is very commonly employed for the mode of existence itself.

IV. *State* is a term nearly synonymous with mode, but of a meaning more extensive, as not exclusively limited to the mutable and contingent.

V. *Quality* is, likewise, a word of a wider signification, for there are essential and accidental qualities. (1.) The *essential* qualities of a thing are those aptitudes, those manners of existence and action, which it cannot lose without ceasing to be. For example, in man, the faculties of sense and intelligence ; in body, the dimensions of length, breadth, and thickness ; in God, the attributes of eternity, omniscience, omnipotence, etc. (2.) By *accidental* qualities are meant those aptitudes and manners of existence and action which substances have at one time and not at another, or which they have always, but may lose without ceasing to be. (*a*) For example, of the *transitory* class are the whiteness of a wall, the health which we enjoy, the fineness of the weather, etc. (*b*) Of the *permanent*

3

class are the gravity of bodies, the periodical move‑ ment of the planets, etc.

VI. *Attribute* is a word properly convertible with *quality*, for every quality is an attribute, and every attribute is a quality; but in our language, custom has introduced a certain distinction in their application. Attribute is considered as a word of loftier signifi‑ cance, and is, therefore, conventionally limited to qual‑ ities of a higher application. Thus, for example, it would be felt as indecorous to speak of the qualities of God, and as ridiculous to talk of the attributes of matter.

VII. *Property* is correctly a synonym for peculiar quality; but it is frequently used as coextensive with quality in general.

VIII. *Accident*, on the contrary, is an abbreviated expression for accidental or contingent quality.

(*B*) Terms expressing the unknown Basis of mental Phenomena.

I. The word *mind* is of a more limited application than the term *soul*. In the Greek Philosophy the term ψυχή, *soul*, comprehends, besides the sensitive and rational principle in man, the principle of organic life both in the animal and vegetable kingdoms.

Since Descartes limited psychology to the domain of consciousness, the term *mind* has been rigidly em‑ ployed for the self-knowing principle alone. Mind, therefore, is to be understood as the subject of the various internal phenomena of which we are con‑ scious.

II. The term *subject* (*subjectum*, ὑπόστασις, ὑποκείμενον) is used to denote the unknown basis which lies under the phenomena of which we become aware, whether in our external or internal experience. But the philosophers of mind have, in a manner, usurped and appropriated this expression to themselves. Accordingly in their hands the phrases, *conscious* or *thinking subject*, and *subject* simply, mean precisely the same thing; and custom has prevailed so far that, in psychological discussions, the *subject* is a term now currently employed throughout Europe for the *mind* or *thinking principle*. The utility of this expression is founded on two circumstances. The first is that it affords an adjective; the second, that the terms *subject* and *subjective* have opposing relatives in the terms *object* and *objective*, so that the two pairs of words together enable us to designate the primary and most important analysis and antithesis of philosophy in a more precise and emphatic manner than can be done by any other technical expressions. Subject, we have seen, is a term for that in which the phenomena, revealed to our observation, inhere, — what the schoolmen have designated the *materia in qua*. Limited to the mental phenomena, *subject*, therefore, denotes the mind itself; and *subjective*, that which belongs to, or proceeds from, the thinking subject. *Object*, on the other hand, is a term for that about which the knowing subject is conversant, — what the schoolmen have styled the *materia circa quam;* while *objective* means that which belongs to, or proceeds from, the object known; and thus denotes what is real in opposition to what is ideal, — what exists in nature in contrast to what exists merely in the thought of the individual.

III. The terms *self* and *ego* we shall take together, as

they are absolutely convertible. The self, the I, is recognized in every act of intelligence, as the subject to which that act belongs. It is I that perceive, I that imagine, I that remember, I that attend, I that compare, I that feel, I that desire, I that will, I that am conscious. The I, indeed, is only manifested in one or other of these special modes; but it is manifested in them all; they are all only the phenomena of the I, and, therefore, the science conversant about the phenomena of mind is, most simply and unambiguously, said to be conversant about the phenomena of the *I* or *Ego.* This expression, as that which, in many relations, best marks and discriminates the conscious mind, has now become familiar in every country, with the exception of our own. Why it has not been naturalized with us is not unapparent. In English *the I* could not be tolerated; because, in sound, it would not be distinguished from the word significant of the organ of sight. We must, therefore, either renounce the term, or resort to the Latin *Ego;* and this is perhaps no disadvantage, for, as the word is only employed in a strictly philosophical relation, it is better that this should be distinctly marked, by its being used in that relation alone. The term *self* is more allowable; yet still the expressions *Ego* and *Non-Ego* are felt to be less awkward than those of *Self* and *Not-Self.* (*Lectures on Metaphysics,* VIII. and IX.)

CHAPTER II.

In taking a comprehensive survey of the mental phenomena, these are all seen to comprise one essential element, or to be possible only under one necessary condition. This element or condition is consciousness, or the knowledge that I, — that the Ego exists, in some determinate state. In this knowledge they appear or are realized as phenomena, and with this knowledge they likewise disappear, or have no longer a phenomenal existence; so that consciousness may be compared to an internal light, by means of which, and which alone, what passes in the mind is rendered visible. It follows, therefore, that consciousness must form the first object of our consideration.

§ 1.   *CONSCIOUSNESS: ITS GENERAL NATURE.*

Nothing has contributed more to spread obscurity over a very transparent matter than the attempts of philosophers to define consciousness. Consciousness cannot be defined; we may be ourselves fully aware what consciousness is, but we cannot, without confusion, convey to others a definition of what we ourselves clearly apprehend. The reason is plain.

Consciousness lies at the root of all knowledge. Consciousness is itself the one highest source of all comprehensibility and illustration; how, then, can we find aught else by which consciousness may be illustrated or comprehended? To accomplish this, it would be necessary to have a second consciousness, through which we might be conscious of the mode in which the first consciousness was possible. In short, the notion of consciousness is so elementary, that it cannot possibly be resolved into others more simple. It cannot, therefore, be brought under any genus, — any more general conception; and, consequently, it cannot be defined. But though consciousness cannot be logically defined, it may, however, be philosophically analyzed. This analysis is effected by observing and holding fast the phenomena or facts of consciousness, comparing these, and, from this comparison, evolving the universal conditions under which alone an act of consciousness is possible.

But before proceeding to show you in detail what the act of consciousness comprises, it may be proper, in the first place, to recall to you, in general, what kind of act the word is employed to denote. I know, I feel, I desire, etc. What is it that is necessarily involved in all these? It requires only to be stated to be admitted, that when I know, I must know that I know, — when I feel, I must know that I feel, — when I desire, I must know that I desire. The knowledge, the feeling, the desire, are possible only under the condition of being known, and being known by me. For if I did not know that I knew, I would not know; if I did not know that I felt, I would not feel; if I did not know that I desired, I would not desire. Now, this knowledge, which I, the subject, have of these modifications of my being, and through which knowledge alone these modifications are possible, is what we call *consciousness*. The expressions *I know that I know; I know that I feel; I know that I desire;* are thus translated by, *I am conscious that I know; I am conscious that I feel; I am conscious that I desire.* Consciousness is thus, on the one hand, the recognition by the mind or ego, of its acts and affections; — in other words, the self-affirmation that certain modifications are known by me, and that these modifications are mine. But, on the other hand, consciousness is not to be viewed as anything different from these modifications themselves, but is, in fact, the general condition of their existence, or of their existence within the sphere of intelligence. Though the simplest act of mind, consciousness thus expresses a relation subsisting between two terms. These terms are, on the one hand, an I or Self, as the subject of a certain modification; and, on the other hand, some modification, state, quality, affection, or operation belonging to the subject. Consciousness, thus, in its simplicity, necessarily involves three things, — (1.) a recognizing or knowing subject; (2.) a recognized or known modification; and (3.) a recognition or knowledge by the subject of the modification.

We may, therefore, lay it down as the most general characteristic of consciousness, that it is *the recognition by the thinking subject of its own acts or affections.*

§ 2. *CONSCIOUSNESS: ITS SPECIAL CONDITIONS.*

In this, the most general characteristic of consciousness, all philosophers are agreed. The more
arduous task remains of determining its special conditions. Of these, likewise, some are almost too
palpable to admit of controversy.

(*A*) Before proceeding to those in regard to which
there is any doubt or difficulty, it will be proper, in
the first place, to state and to dispose of such determinations as are too palpable to be called in question.
Of these admitted limitations,

I. The first is, that consciousness is *an actual and
not a potential knowledge.* Thus a man is said to
know, that is, is able to know, that $7 + 9$ are $= 16$,
though that equation be not, at the moment, the
object of thought; but we cannot say that he is conscious of this truth unless while it is actually present
to his mind.

II. The second limitation is, that consciousness is
an immediate, not a mediate knowledge. We are said,
for example, to know a past occurrence when we
represent it to the mind in an act of memory. We
know the mental representation, and this we do immediately and in itself, and are also said to know the
past occurrence, as mediately knowing it through the
mental modification which represents it. Now, we
are conscious of the representation as immediately
known ; but we cannot be said to be conscious of the
thing represented, which, if known, is only known
through its representation.

III. The third condition of consciousness, which may be held as universally admitted, is, that it supposes *a contrast, — a discrimination;* for we can be conscious only inasmuch as we are conscious of something; and we are conscious of something only inasmuch as we are conscious of what that something is, — that is, distinguish it from what it is not. This discrimination is of different kinds and degrees. (1.) In the first place, there is the contrast between the two grand opposites, self and not-self, — ego and non-ego, — mind and matter. We are conscious of self only in and by its contradistinction from not-self; and are conscious of not-self only in and by its contradistinction from self. (2.) In the second place, there is the discrimination of the states or modifications of the internal subject or self from each other. We are conscious of one mental state only as we contradistinguish it from another; where two, three, or more such states are confounded, we are conscious of them as one; and were we to note no difference in our mental modifications, we might be said to be absolutely unconscious. (3.) In the third place, there is the distinction between the parts and qualities of the outer world. We are conscious of an external object only as we are conscious of it as distinct from others; where several distinguishable objects are confounded, we are conscious of them as one; where no object is discriminated, we are not conscious of any.[1]

IV. The fourth condition of consciousness, which

---

[1] See this subject treated more fully under *Phenomenology of the Cognitions*, Chap. V., § 1.

may be assumed as very generally acknowledged, is, that it involves *judgment*.[1] A judgment is the mental act by which one thing is affirmed or denied of another. This fourth condition is in truth only a necessary consequence of the third, — for it is impossible to discriminate without judging, discrimination or contradistinction being, in fact, only the denying one thing of another.

V. The fifth undeniable condition of consciousness is *memory*. This condition also is a corollary of the third. For without memory our mental states could not be held fast, compared, distinguished from each other, and referred to self. Without memory, each indivisible, each infinitesimal, moment in the mental succession would stand isolated from each other, — would constitute, in fact, a separate existence. The notion of the ego, or self, arises from the recognized permanence and identity of the thinking subject in contrast to the recognized succession and variety of its modifications. But this recognition is possible only through memory. The notion of self is, therefore, the result of memory. But the notion of self is involved in consciousness, so consequently is memory. (*Lect. on Metaph.*, XI. Compare *Reid's Works*, pp. 932-7.)

(*B*) We are now about to enter on a more disputed. territory. Aristotle, Descartes, Locke, and philosophers in general, have regarded consciousness, not as a particular faculty, but as the universal condition of intelligence. Reid, on the contrary, following, probably, Hutcheson, and followed by Stewart, Royer-

---

[1] See note on preceding page.

Collard, and others, has classed consciousness as a co-ordinate faculty with the other intellectual powers; distinguished from them, not as the species from the individual, but as the individual from the individual. And as the particular faculties have each their peculiar object, so the peculiar object of consciousness is the *operations of the other faculties themselves, to the exclusion of the objects* about which these operations are conversant.

This analysis we regard as false.[1] For it is impossible, in the *first* place, to discriminate consciousness from all the other cognitive faculties, or to discriminate any one of these from consciousness; and, in the *second*, to conceive a faculty cognizant of the various mental operations, without being also cognizant of their several objects.

I. *We know*, and *We know that we know:* — these propositions, *logically* distinct, are *really* identical; each implies the other. We *know* (i. e., feel, perceive, imagine, remember, etc.) only as we *know that we thus know;* and we *know that we know*, only as we know in *some particular manner* (i. e., *feel, perceive,* etc.). So true is the scholastic brocard : "*Non sentimus nisi sentiamus nos sentire; non sentimus nos sentire nisi sentiamus.*" The attempt to analyze the

---

[1] This is described by Hamilton as "the *first* contested position," which he intends to maintain, with regard to consciousness (*Lect. on Metaph.*, p. 143, *Am. ed.*); but it leads him into a long digression (*Ibid.*, pp. 143–182), at the close of which there is no mention of any other contested positions. Did this digression cause him to forget his apparent intention to continue the subject from which he started? His editors give no indication that they have observed this omission. — J. C. M.

cognition *I know*, and the cognition *I know that I know*, into the separate energies of distinct faculties, is therefore vain. But this is the analysis of Reid. Consciousness, which the formula *I know that I know* adequately expresses, he views as a power specifically distinct from the various cognitive faculties comprehended under the formula *I know*, precisely as these faculties are severally contradistinguished from each other. But here the parallel does not hold. I can feel without perceiving; I can perceive without imagining; I can imagine without remembering; I can remember without judging (in the emphatic signification); I can judge without willing. One of these acts does not immediately suppose the other. Though modes merely of the same indivisible subject, they are modes in *relation to each other*, really distinct, and admit, therefore, of psychological discrimination. But can I feel without being conscious that I feel? — can I remember without being conscious that I remember? or, can I be conscious without being conscious that I perceive, or imagine, or reason, — that I energize, in short, in some determinate mode, which Reid would view as the act of a faculty specifically different from consciousness? That this is impossible Reid himself admits. But if, on the one hand, consciousness be only realized under specific modes, and cannot therefore exist apart from the several faculties *in cumulo;* and if, on the other, these faculties can all and each only be exerted under the condition of consciousness; consciousness, consequently, is not one of the special modes into which our mental activity may be resolved, but the fundamental form, — the generic condition of them all. Every intelligent act is thus a modified consciousness; and consciousness a comprehensive term for the complement of our cognitive energies.

II. But the vice of Reid's analysis is further manifested in his arbitrary limitation of the sphere of consciousness; proposing to it the various intellectual operations, but excluding their objects. "I am conscious," he says, "of perception, but not of the object I perceive; I am conscious of memory, but not of the object I remember."

The reduction of consciousness to a particular faculty entailed this limitation. For, once admitting consciousness to be cognizant of *objects* as of *operations*, Reid could not, without absurdity, degrade it to the level of a special power. For thus, in the *first* place, consciousness, coextensive with *all* our cognitive faculties, would yet be made co-ordinate with *each;* and in the *second*, two faculties would be supposed to be simultaneously exercised about the same object, to the same extent.

But the alternative which Reid has chosen is, at least, equally untenable. The assertion that we can be conscious of an act of knowledge without being conscious of its object, is virtually suicidal. A mental operation is only what it is by relation to its object; the object at once determining its existence, and specifying the character of its existence. But if a relation cannot be comprehended in one of its terms, so we cannot be conscious of an operation without being conscious of the object to which it exists only as correlative. For example, We are conscious of a perception, says Reid, but are not conscious of its object. Yet how can we be conscious of a *perception*, that is, how can we *know* that a perception exists, — that it is a perception, and not another mental state, — and that it is the perception of a rose, and of nothing but a rose; unless this *consciousness* involve a knowledge (or consciousness) of the object which at once determines the existence of an act, specifies its kind, and distinguishes its individuality? Annihilate the object, you annihilate the operation; annihilate the consciousness of the object, you annihilate the consciousness of the operation. In the greater number indeed of our cognitive energies, the two terms of the relation of knowledge exist only as identical; the object admitting only of a logical discrimination from the subject. I imagine a Hippogryph. The Hippogryph is at once the object of the act and the act itself. Abstract the one, the other has no existence; deny me the consciousness of the Hippogryph, you deny me the consciousness of the imagination; I am conscious of zero; I am not conscious at all. (*Discussions*, pp. 47–49. Compare *Lect. on Metaph.*, XII.)

§ 3. CONSCIOUSNESS: ITS EVIDENCE AND AUTHORITY.

I now proceed to consider consciousness as the source from whence we must derive every fact in the Philosophy of Mind. And in prosecution of this purpose I shall, in the *first* place, endeavor to show you that it really is the principal, if not the only, source from which all knowledge of the mental phenomena must be obtained; and, in the *second* place, I shall consider the character of its evidence, and what, under different relations, are the degrees of its authority.

(A) As consciousness has been shown to be the condition of all the mental phenomena, it is mainly, if not solely, to consciousness, that we must resort for an acquaintance with these phenomena. According to the doctrine of phrenology, indeed, an acquaintance with the various mental powers may be obtained by observation of the various parts of the brain, which that science maintains that it has discovered to be their several organs. But though the mind, in its lower energies and affections, is immediately dependent on the conditions of the nervous system, and, in general, the development of the brain in different species of animals is correspondent to their intelligence, still it is impossible to connect the mind or its faculties with particular parts of the nervous system. For I have proved, by the most extensive induction, that the alleged physiological facts on which phrenology professes to be based, such as its assertion of the correspondence between the development of the cerebellum and the function which it ascribes to it, are often not only unfounded, but the very reverse of the truth.[1]

---

[1] In the above paragraph I have endeavored to embody the teaching of Sir William Hamilton on the subject of which it treats. His editors have relegated this portion of his lectures, so far as it seemed worthy of preservation, to an appendix (*Lect. on Metaph.*, Appendix II.), where it may be consulted. I have thought it unnecessary to go into detail, both because the position of phrenology has changed since Hamilton's time, and because it is unnecessary to digress into the question concerning the function of the various organs in the

(*B*) We proceed to consider, in the next place, the authority, the certainty, of this instrument.

Now, it is at once evident, that philosophy, as it affirms its own possibility, must affirm the veracity of consciousness; for, as philosophy is only a scientific development of the facts which consciousness reveals, it follows, that philosophy, in denying or doubting the testimony of consciousness, would deny or doubt its own existence. (*Lect. on Metaph.*, XV.) How, then, do the facts of consciousness certify us of their own veracity? To this the only possible answer is, that as elements of our mental constitution, as the essential conditions of our knowledge, they *must* by us be accepted as true. To suppose their falsehood, is to suppose that we are created capable of intelligence, in order to be made the victims of delusion; that God is a deceiver, and the root of our nature a lie. But such a supposition, if gratuitous, is manifestly illegitimate. For, on the contrary, the data of our original consciousness must, it is evident, *in the first instance*, be presumed true. It is only if proved false, that their authority can, *in consequence of that proof*, be, in the second instance, disallowed.

Here, however, at the outset, it is proper to take a distinction, the neglect of which has been productive of considerable error and confusion. It is the distinction between the data or deliverances of consciousness considered simply *in themselves, as appre-*

encephalon, in order to vindicate, not only the value, but the necessity, of reflection in the study of mind. — J. C. M.

hended facts or actual manifestations, and those deliverances considered *as testimonies to the truth of facts beyond their own phenomenal reality.*

I. Viewed under the former limitation, they are above all scepticism. For as doubt is itself only a manifestation of consciousness, it is impossible to doubt that, when consciousness manifests, it does manifest, without, in thus doubting, doubting that we actually doubt; that is, without the doubt contradicting and therefore annihilating itself. Hence it is that the facts of consciousness, as mere phenomena, are by the unanimous confession of all sceptics and idealists, ancient and modern, placed high above the reach of question.

II. Viewed under the latter limitation, the deliverances of consciousness do not thus peremptorily repel even the possibility of doubt. I am conscious, for example, in an act of sensible perception, (1.) of myself, the subject knowing; and, (2.) of something given as different from myself, the object known. To take the second term of this relation: that I am conscious in this act of an object given, *as a non-ego,* — that is, *as not a modification of my mind,* — of this, *as a phenomenon,* doubt is impossible. For, as has been seen, we cannot doubt the actuality of a fact of consciousness without doubting, that is subverting, our doubt itself. To this extent, therefore, all scepticism is precluded. But though it cannot but be admitted that the object of which we are conscious in this cognition is given, not *as* a mode of self, but *as* a mode of something different from self, it is, however, possible for us to suppose, without our supposi-

4

tion, at least, being *felo-de-se*, that, though *given as* a non-ego, this object may, *in reality*, *be* only a *representation* of a *non-ego*, in and by the *ego*. Let this, therefore, be maintained; let the *fact* of the testimony be admitted, but the *truth* of the testimony, to aught beyond its own ideal existence, be doubted or denied. How in this case are we to proceed? It is evident that the doubt does not in this, as in the former case, refute itself. It is not suicidal by self-contradiction. The Idealist, therefore, in denying the existence of an external world, as more than a subjective phenomenon of the internal, does not advance a doctrine *ab initio* null, as a scepticism would be which denied the phenomena of the internal world itself.

It is, therefore, manifest that we may throw wholly out of account the phenomena of consciousness, considered merely in themselves; seeing that scepticism in regard to them, under this limitation, is confessedly impossible; and that it is only requisite to vindicate the truth of these phenomena, viewed as attestations of more than their own existence, seeing that they are not, in this respect, placed beyond the possibility of doubt.

When, for example, consciousness assures us that, in perception, we are immediately cognizant of an external and extended non-ego; or that, in remembrance, through the imagination, of which we are immediately cognizant, we obtain a mediate knowledge of a real past; how shall we repel the doubt, — in the former case, that what is given as the extended reality itself is not merely a representation of matter by mind; in the latter, that what is given as a mediate knowledge of

the past, is not a mere phantasm, containing an illu-
sive reference to an unreal past? We can do this
only in one way. The legitimacy of such gratuitous
doubt necessarily supposes that the deliverance of
consciousness *is not to be presumed true.* If, therefore, it can be shown, on the one hand, that the deliverances of consciousness must philosophically be
accepted, *until* their certain or probable falsehood has
been positively evinced; and if, on the other hand,
it cannot be shown that any attempt to discredit the
veracity of consciousness has ever yet succeeded; it
follows that, as philosophy now stands, the testimony
of consciousness must be viewed as high above suspicion, and its declarations entitled to demand prompt
and unconditional assent.

I. In the first place, as has been said, it cannot but
be acknowledged that the veracity of consciousness
must, at least in the first instance, be conceded.
" *Neganti incumbit probatio.*" Nature is not gratui-
tously to be assumed to work, not only in vain, but
in counteraction of herself; our faculty of knowledge
is not without a ground to be supposed an instrument
of illusion; man, unless the melancholy fact be proved,
is not to be held organized for the attainment, and
actuated by the love of truth, only to become the
dupe and victim of a perfidious creator.

II. But, in the second place, though the veracity
of the primary convictions of consciousness must, in
the outset, be admitted, it still remains competent to
lead a proof that they are undeserving of credit. But
how is this to be done? As the ultimate grounds of
knowledge, these convictions cannot be redargued

from any higher knowledge; and as original beliefs, they are. paramount in certainty to every derivative assurance. But they are many; they are, in authority, co-ordinate; and their testimony is clear and precise. It is therefore competent for us to view them in correlation; to compare their declarations, and to consider whether they contradict, and, by contradicting, invalidate each other. This mutual contradiction is possible in two ways. (1.) It may be that the *primary data themselves* are directly or immediately contradictory of each other; (2.) It may be that they are mediately or indirectly contradictory, inasmuch as the *consequences* to which they *necessarily* lead, and for the truth or falsehood of which they are therefore responsible, are mutually repugnant. By evincing either of these, the veracity of consciousness will be disproved; for in either case consciousness is shown to be inconsistent with itself, and consequently inconsistent with the unity of truth. But by no other process of demonstration is this possible. (*Reid's Works*, pp. 743–5.)

Before we are entitled to accuse consciousness of being a false witness, we are bound, first of all, to see whether there be any rules by which, in employing the testimony of consciousness, we must be governed; and whether philosophers have evolved their systems out of consciousness in obedience to these rules. For if there be rules under which alone the evidence of consciousness can be fairly and fully given, and, consequently, under which alone consciousness can serve as an infallible standard of certainty and truth, and if philosophers have despised or neglected these,

then must we remove the reproach from the instrument, and affix it to those blundering workmen who
have not known how to handle and apply it. Now,
in attempting a scientific deduction of the philosophy
of mind from the facts of consciousness, there are, in
all, if I generalize correctly, three laws which afford
the exclusive conditions of psychological legitimacy.

I. *The Law of Parcimony:* That we admit nothing
which is not either an original datum of consciousness
or the legitimate consequence of such a datum.

II. *The Law of Integrity:* That we embrace all
the original data of consciousness and all their legitimate consequences.

III. *The Law of Harmony:* That we exhibit each
of these in its individual integrity, neither distorted
nor mutilated, and in its relative place, whether of
pre-eminence or subordination. (*Lect. on Metaph.*,
XV., and *Reid's Works*, p. 747.)

§ 4. CONSCIOUSNESS: CLASSIFICATION OF ITS PHE-NOMENA.

On taking a survey of the mental modifications or
phenomena of which we are conscious, these are seen
to divide themselves into three great classes. (1.) In
the first place, there are the phenomena of Knowledge ;
(2.) In the second place, there are the phenomena of
Feeling, or the phenomena of pleasure and pain ; and
(3.) In the third place, there are the phenomena of
Conation, or of will and desire. Let me illustrate
this by an example. I see a picture. Now, first of
all, I am conscious of perceiving a certain com-

plement of colors and figures ; I recognize what the object is. This is the phenomenon of *Cognition* or *Knowledge*. But this is not the only phenomenon of which I may be here conscious. I may experience certain affections in the contemplation of this object. If the picture be a masterpiece, the gratification will be unalloyed; but if it be an unequal production, I shall be conscious, perhaps of enjoyment, but of enjoyment alloyed with dissatisfaction. This is the phenomenon of *Feeling*, or of *Pleasure and Pain*. But these two phenomena do not yet exhaust all of which I may be conscious on the occasion. I may desire to see the picture long, — to see it often, — to make it my own, and, perhaps, I may will, resolve, or determine so to do. This is the complex phenomenon of *Will and Desire*. The characters by which these three classes are reciprocally discriminated, are the following : —

I. In the phenomena of cognition, consciousness distinguishes an object known from the subject knowing. This object may be of two kinds : it may either be the quality of something different from the ego ; or it may be a modification of the ego or subject itself. In the former case, the object, which may be called for the sake of discrimination the *object-object*, is given as something different from the percipient subject. In the latter case, the object, which may be called the *subject-object*, is given as really identical with the conscious ego ; but still consciousness distinguishes it, as an accident, from the ego. As the subject of that accident, it projects, as it were, this subjective phenomenon from itself, — views it at a distance, — in a word, objectifies it. This discrimination of self from self — this objectification — is the quality which constitutes the essential peculiarity of cognition.

II. In the phenomena of feeling, on the contrary, consciousness does not place the mental modification or state beyond itself; it does not contemplate it apart, — as separate from itself, — but is, as it were, fused into one. The peculiarity of feeling, therefore, is that there is nothing but what is subjectively subjective; there is no object different from self, — no objectification of any mode of self. We are, indeed, able to constitute our states of pain and pleasure into objects of reflection; but in so far as they are objects of reflection, they are not feelings, but only reflex cognitions of feelings.

III. In the phenomena of conation, there is, as in those of cognition, an object, and this object is also an object of knowledge. Will and desire are only possible through knowledge, — "*Ignoti nulla cupido.*" But though both cognition and conation bear relation to an object, they are discriminated by the difference of this relation itself. In cognition, there exists no want; and the object, whether objective or subjective, is not sought for, nor avoided; whereas in conation there is a want, and a tendency supposed, which results in an endeavor, either to obtain the object, when the cognitive faculties represent it as fitted to afford the fruition of the want; or to ward off the object, if these faculties represent it as calculated to frustrate the tendency of its accomplishment. (*Lect. on Metaph.*, XLII.)

To the above classification of the mental phenomena objections have been taken.

I. It has been objected, that the three classes are co-ordinate. It is evident that every mental phenomenon is either an act of knowledge, or only possible through an act of knowledge, for consciousness is a knowledge, and, on this principle, many philosophers, as Descartes, Leibnitz, Spinoza, Wolf, Platner, and others, have been led to regard the faculty of cognition as the fundamental power of mind, from which all others are derivative. To this the answer is easy. These philosophers did not observe that, although pleasure and pain, although desire and volition, are only as they are known to be; yet, in these modifications, a quality, a phenomenon of mind, absolutely new, has been superadded, which was never involved in, and could, therefore, never have been evolved out of, the mere faculty of knowledge. The faculty of knowledge is certainly the first in order, inasmuch as it is the *conditio sine qua non* of the others; and we are able to conceive a being possessed of the power of recognizing existence, and yet wholly void of all feeling of pain and pleasure, and of all powers of desire and volition. On the other hand, we are wholly unable to conceive a being possessed of feeling and desire, and, at the same time, without a knowledge of any object upon which his affections may be employed, and without a consciousness of these affections themselves.

We can farther conceive a being possessed of knowledge and feeling alone, — a being endowed with a power of recognizing objects, of enjoying the exercise, and of grieving at the restraint of his activity, — and yet devoid of voluntary agency — of that conation which is possessed by man. To such a being would belong feelings of pain and pleasure, but neither desire nor will, properly so called. On the other hand, however, we cannot possibly conceive the existence of a voluntary activity independently of all feeling; for voluntary conation is a faculty which can only be determined to energy through a pain or pleasure, — through an estimate of the relative worth of objects.

In distinguishing the cognitions, feelings, and conations, it is not, therefore, to be supposed that these phenomena are possible independently of each other. In our philosophical systems, they may stand separated from each other in books and chapters; in nature, they are ever interwoven. In every, the simplest, modification of mind, knowledge, feeling, and desire or will, go to constitute the mental state; and it is only by a scientific abstraction that we are able to analyze the state into elements, which are never really existent but in mutual combination. These elements are found, indeed, in very various proportions in different states; sometimes one preponderates, sometimes another; but there is no state in which they are not all coexistent. (*Lect. on Metaph.*, XI.)

II. A second objection is urged by Krug, a distinguished champion of the Kantian system, who goes so far as to maintain, not only that what have obtained the name of *feelings* constitute no distinct class of mental functions, but that the very supposition is absurd, and even impossible. The power of cognition and the power of conation, he holds, are in propriety to be regarded as two different fundamental powers, only because the operation of our mind exhibits a twofold direction of its whole activity, — one inwards, another outwards; in consequence of which we are constrained to distinguish, on the one hand, an *immanent* ideal or theoretical, and, on the other, a *transeunt* real or practical, activity. Hence it is argued that, if we interpolate a third species of activity, its direction must be either immanent or transeunt, or both, or neither of these; but on the first three suppositions there are still only two kinds of mental activity, and on the fourth there is merely an additional activity, in no direction, which is no activity at all. In answer to this it may be said, (1.) That, in place of two forms of mental activity, we may competently suppose three, *ineunt, immanent,* and *transeunt.* (2.) That directions are properly ascribed only to the movements of external things. (Abridged from Lecture XLI. of the *Lect. on Metaph.*)

The order of these phenomena is determined by their relative consecution. Feeling and appetency suppose knowledge. The cognitive faculties, therefore, stand first. But as will, and desire, and aversion suppose a knowledge of the pleasurable and painful, the feelings will stand second as intermediate between the other two. (*Lect. on Metaph.*, XI.) The phenomena of knowledge come, therefore, first under consideration, and philosophy is principally and primarily the *Science of Knowledge.* (*Reid's Works,* p. 808, note.)

FIRST PART OF PHENOMENAL PSYCHOLOGY.

PHENOMENOLOGY OF THE COGNITIONS.

INTRODUCTION.

CLASSIFICATION OF THE COGNITIVE FACULTIES.

I now proceed to the particular investigation of the first class of the mental phenomena, and shall commence by delineating to you the distribution of the cognitive faculties which I shall adopt, — a distribution different from any other with which I am acquainted. But I would first premise an observation in regard to psychological powers.

As to mental powers, you are not to suppose them entities really distinguishable from the thinking principle, or really different from each other. Mental powers are not like bodily organs. It is the same simple substance which exerts every energy of every faculty, however various, and which is affected in every mode of every capacity, however opposite.

It is a fact, too notorious to be denied, that the mind is capable of different modifications; that is, can exert different actions, and can be affected by different passions. But these actions and passions are not all dissimilar; every action and passion is not different from every other. On the contrary, they are like, and they are unlike. Those, therefore, that are like, we group or assort together in thought, and bestow on them a common name; nor are these groups or assortments manifold, — they are, in fact, few and simple. Again, every action is an effect; every action and passion a modification. But every effect supposes a cause; every modification supposes a subject. When we say that the mind exerts an energy, we virtually say that the mind is the cause of the energy; when we say that the mind acts or suffers, we say, in other words, that the mind is the subject of a modification. But the modifications, that is, the actions and passions, of the mind, as we stated, all fall into a few resembling groups, which we designate by a peculiar name; and as the mind is the common cause and subject of all these, we are surely entitled to say, in general, that the mind has the faculty of exerting such and such a class of energies, or has the capacity of being modified by such and such an order of affections. On this doctrine, a *faculty* is nothing more than a general term for the causality the mind has of originating a certain class of energies; a *capacity*, only a general term for the susceptibility the mind has of being affected by a particular class of emotions.

From what I have now said, you will be better prepared for what I am about to state in regard to the classification of the first great order of mental phenomena, and the distribution of the faculties of knowledge founded thereon. I formerly told you that the mental phenomena are never presented to us sepa-

rately; they are always in conjunction, and it is only
by an ideal analysis and abstraction that, for the purposes of science, they can be discriminated and considered apart. The problem, proposed in such an
analysis, is to find the primary threads which, in their
composition, form the complex tissue of thought. In
what ought to be accomplished by such an analysis,
all philosophers are agreed, however different may
have been the result of their attempts. I shall not
state and criticise the various classifications pro-
pounded of the cognitive faculties. I shall only de-
lineate the distribution of the faculties of knowledge
which I have adopted, and endeavor to afford you
some general insight into its principles.

I again repeat that consciousness constitutes, or is
coextensive with, all our faculties of knowledge, —
these faculties being only special modifications under
which consciousness is manifested. It being, therefore, understood that consciousness is not a special
faculty of knowledge, but the general faculty out of
which the special faculties of knowledge are evolved,
I proceed to this evolution.

I. In the first place, as we are endowed with a faculty of Cognition, or Consciousness in general, and
since it cannot be maintained that we have always
possessed the knowledge which we now possess, it
will be admitted that we must have a faculty of acquiring knowledge. But this acquisition of knowledge can only be accomplished by the immediate
presentation of a new object to consciousness; in other
words, by the reception of a new object within the
sphere of our cognition. We have thus a faculty

which may be called the *Acquisitive,* or the *Presenta-tive,* or the *Receptive.*

Now, new or adventitious knowledge may be either of things external or of things internal. If the object of knowledge be external, the faculty receptive or presentative of the qualities of such object will be a consciousness of the non-ego. This has obtained the name of *External Perception,* or of *Perception* simply. If, on the other hand, the object be internal, the faculty receptive or presentative of the qualities of such subject-object, will be a consciousness of the ego. This faculty obtains the name of *Internal* or *Reflex Perception,* or of *Self-consciousness.* By the foreign psychologists this faculty is termed also the *Internal Sense.*

II. In the second place, inasmuch as we are capable of knowledge, we must be endowed not only with a faculty of acquiring, but with a faculty of retaining or conserving it when acquired. We have thus, as a second necessary faculty, one that may be called the *Conservative* or *Retentive.* This is *Memory,* strictly so denominated.

III. But, in the third place, if we are capable of knowledge, it is not enough that we possess a faculty of acquiring, and a faculty of retaining it in the mind, but out of consciousness; we must further be endowed with a faculty of recalling it out of unconsciousness into consciousness; in short, a reproductive power. This *Reproductive* faculty is governed by the laws which regulate the succession of our thoughts, — the laws, as they are called, of Mental Association. If these laws are allowed to operate without the intervention of the will, this faculty may be called *Suggestion*, or *Spontaneous Suggestion;* — whereas, if applied under the influence of the will, it will properly obtain the name of *Reminiscence*, or *Recollection*. By reproduction, it should be observed, that I strictly mean the process of recovering the absent thought from unconsciousness, and not its representation in consciousness.

IV. In the fourth place, as capable of knowledge, we must not only be endowed with a presentative, a conservative, and a reproductive faculty ; there is required for their consummation a faculty of representing in consciousness, and of keeping before the mind the knowledge presented, retained, and reproduced. We have thus a *Representative* faculty ; and this obtains the name of *Imagination* or *Phantasy*.

V. In the fifth place, all the faculties we have considered are only subsidiary. They acquire, preserve, call out, and hold up, the materials, for the use of a higher faculty which operates upon these materials, and which we may call the *Elaborative* or *Discursive* faculty. This faculty has only one operation,— it only compares. It may startle you to hear that the highest function of mind is nothing higher than comparison; but, in the end, I am confident of convincing you of the paradox.

VI. But, in the sixth and last place, the mind is not altogether indebted to experience for the whole apparatus of its knowledge. What we know by experience, without experience we should not have known ; and as all our experience is contingent, all the knowledge derived from experience is contingent also. But

5

there are cognitions in the mind which are not contingent, — which are necessary, — which we cannot but think, — which thought supposes as its fundamental condition. These cognitions, therefore, are not mere generalizations from experience. But if not derived from experience, they must be native to the mind. These native cognitions are the laws by which the mind is governed in its operations, and which afford the conditions of its capacity of knowledge. These necessary laws, or primary conditions of intelligence, are phenomena of a similar character; and we must, therefore, generalize or collect them into a class; and on the power possessed by the mind of manifesting these phenomena we may bestow the name of the *Regulative* faculty. (*Lect. on Metaph.*, XX.)

The following is a tabular view of the distribution of the Special Faculties of Knowledge.

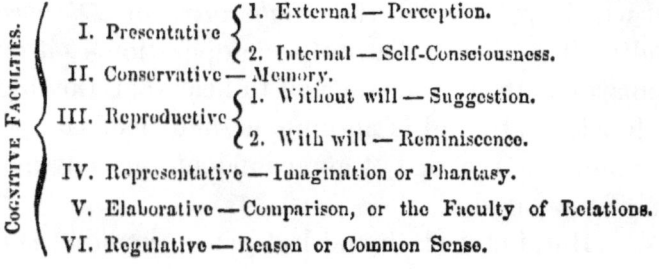

PHENOMENOLOGY OF THE COGNITIONS.

CHAPTER I.

THE PRESENTATIVE FACULTY.

This faculty is subdivided into *External Perception* and *Internal Perception*, or Self-consciousness. I commence with the former of these.

§ 1. *EXTERNAL PERCEPTION.*

External or *Sensitive Perception*, or *Perception* simply,[1] is that act of consciousness whereby we apprehend in our body, (1.) certain *special affections*, whereof, as an *animated* organism, it is contingently susceptible; and (2.) those *general relations of extension*, under which, as a *material* organism, it necessarily exists. Of these perceptions the former is *sensation proper;* the latter, *perception proper.* (*Reid's Works*, pp. 876–7.) This distinction it is necessary to explain, as well as a correlative distinction in the qualities of matter; and we shall thus be the better

---

[1] For a sketch of the various meanings of the word Perception, see *Reid's Works*, p. 876, note. — J. C. M.

prepared for understanding the true theory of perception.

(*A*) SENSATION AND PERCEPTION. Before proceeding to state the great law which regulates the mutual relation of these phenomena, it is proper to say a few words illustrative of the nature of the phenomena themselves. Perception is a special kind of knowledge; sensation a special kind of feeling; and *Knowledge* and *Feeling*, it will be remembered, are two out of the three great classes, into which we divided the phenomena of mind. Now, as Perception is only a special mode of Knowledge, and Sensation only a special mode of Feeling, so the contrast of Perception and Sensation is only the special manifestation of a contrast, which universally divides the generic phenomena themselves. It ought, therefore, in the first place, to have been noticed, that the generic phenomena of Knowledge and Feeling are always found coexistent, and yet always distinct; and the opposition of Perception and Sensation should have been stated as an obtrusive, but still only a particular, example of the general law. But not only is the distinction of Perception and Sensation not generalized by our psychologists; it is not concisely and precisely stated. A Cognition is *objective*, that is, our consciousness is then relative to something different from the present state of the mind itself; Feeling, on the contrary, is *subjective*, that is, our consciousness is exclusively limited to the pleasure or pain experienced by the thinking subject. Cognition and feeling are always coexistent. The purest act of knowledge is always colored by some feeling of pleasure or pain;

for no energy is absolutely indifferent, and the grossest feeling exists only as it is known in consciousness. This being the case of cognition and feeling in general, the same is true of perception and sensation in particular. (Perception proper is the consciousness, through the senses, of the qualities of an object known as different from self;)(Sensation proper is the consciousness of the subjective affection of pleasure or pain, which accompanies that act of knowledge.) Perception is thus the objective element in the complex state, — the element of Cognition; Sensation is the subjective element, — the element of Feeling.

The most remarkable defect, however, in the present doctrine upon this point, is the ignorance of our psychologists in regard to the law by which the phenomena of cognition and feeling, — of perception and sensation, — are governed, in their reciprocal relation. This law is simple and universal; and, once enounced, its proof is found in every mental manifestation. It is this: *Knowledge and Feeling, — Perception and Sensation, — though always coexistent, are always in the inverse ratio of each other.* That these two elements are always found in coexistence, as it is an old and a notorious truth, it is not requisite for me to prove. But that these elements are always found to coexist in an inverse proportion, — in support of this universal fact, it will be requisite to adduce proof and illustration.

In doing this I shall, however, confine myself to the relation of Perception and Sensation.

I. The first proof I shall take from a comparison of the *several senses;* and it will be found that, (pre-

cisely as a sense has more of the one element, it has less of the other.) Laying Touch aside for the moment, as this requires a special explanation, the other four senses divide themselves into two classes, according as Perception or Sensation predominates. The two in which the former element prevails, are Sight and Hearing; the two in which the latter, are Taste and Smell.

1. Taking the first two, it will be at once admitted that

(*a*) *Sight* at the same instant presents to us a greater number and a greater variety of objects and qualities than any other of the senses. In this sense, therefore, Perception is at its maximum. But Sensation is here at its minimum; for in the eye we experience less organic pleasure or pain from the impressions of its appropriate objects (colors), than we do in any other sense.

(*b*) Next to Sight, *Hearing* affords us, in the shortest interval, the greatest variety and multitude of cognitions; and as sight divides space almost to infinity, through color, so hearing does the same to time, through sound. Hearing is, however, much less extensive in its sphere of Knowledge or Perception than sight; but in the same proportion is its capacity of Feeling or Sensation more intensive. We have greater pleasure and greater pain from single sounds than from single colors; and, in like manner, concords and discords, in the one sense, affect us more agreeably or disagreeably, than any modifications of light in the other.

2. In *Taste* and *Smell* the degree of Sensation,

that is, of pleasure or pain, is great in proportion as the perception, that is, the information they afford, is small.

3. In regard to *Touch*, without entering on disputed questions, it is sufficient to know, that in those parts of the body where sensation predominates, perception is feeble; and in those where perception is lively, sensation is obtuse. In the finger-points tactile perception is at its height; but there is hardly any other part of the body in which sensation is not more acute. Touch, therefore, if viewed as a single sense, belongs to both classes, — the objective and the subjective. But it is more correct to regard it as a plurality of senses, in which case touch, properly so called, having a principal organ in the finger-points, will belong to the class in which perception, proper predominates.

II. The analogy, which we have thus seen to hold good in the several senses in relation to each other, prevails likewise among *the several impressions of the same sense*. Impressions in the same sense differ both (1.) in degree and (2.) in quality or kind.

1. Taking their *difference in degree*, and supposing that the degree of the impression determines the degree of the sensation, it cannot certainly be said, that the minimum of Sensation infers the maximum of Perception; for Perception always supposes a certain quantum of Sensation: but this is undeniable, that, above a certain limit, Perception declines, in proportion as Sensation rises. Thus, in the sense of sight, if the impression be strong we are dazzled, blinded, and consciousness is limited to the pain or

pleasure of the Sensation, in the intensity of which Perception has been lost.

2. Take now the *difference*, *in kind*, of impressions in the same sense. Of the senses, take again that of Sight. Sight, as will hereafter be shown, is cognizant of color, and of figure. But though figure is known only through color, a very imperfect cognizance of color is necessary, as is shown in the case (and it is not a rare one) of those individuals who have not the faculty of discriminating colors. These persons, who probably perceive only a certain difference of light and shade, have as clear and distinct a cognizance of figure, as others who enjoy the sense of sight in absolute perfection. This being understood, you will observe, that, in the vision of color, there is more of Sensation; in that of figure, more of Perception. Color affords our faculties of knowledge a far smaller number of differences and relations than figure; but, at the same time, yields our capacity of feeling a far more sensual enjoyment. But if the pleasure we derive from color be more gross and vivid, that from figure is more refined and permanent. It is a law of our nature, that the more intense a pleasure, the shorter is its duration. The pleasures of sense are grosser and more intense than those of intellect; but, while the former alternate speedily with disgust, with the latter we are never satiated. The same analogy holds among the senses themselves. Those in which Sensation predominates, in which pleasure is most intense, soon pall upon us; whereas those in which Perception predominates, and which hold more immediately of intelligence, afford us a less

exclusive but a more enduring gratification. How soon
are we cloyed with the pleasures of the palate, compared with those of the eye ; and, among the objects
of the former, the meats that please the most are
soonest objects of disgust. This is too notorious in
regard to taste to stand in need of proof. But it is
no less certain in the case of vision. In painting,
there is a pleasure derived from a vivid and harmonious coloring, and a pleasure from the drawing and
grouping of the figures. The two pleasures are distinct, and even, to a certain extent, incompatible.
For if we attempt to combine them, the grosser and
more obtrusive gratification, which we find in the coloring, distracts us from the more refined and intellectual enjoyment we derive from the relation of figure ;
while, at the same time, the disgust we soon experience from the one tends to render us insensible to the
other. (*Lect. on Metaph.*, XXIV.[1])

(*B*) DISTINCTION IN THE QUALITIES OF MATTER.
The qualities of body I divide into three classes.
Adopting and adapting, as far as possible, the previous nomenclature,[2] the first of these I would denominate the class of *Primary*, or *Objective*, Qualities ; the
second, the class of *Secundo-Primary*, or *Subjectivo-
Objective*, Qualities ; the third, the class of *Secondary*,
or *Subjective*, Qualities.

The general point of view from which the Qualities
of Matter are here considered is not the *Physical*, but

---

[1] See also *Reid's Works*, Note D*. This note contains a history of
the recognition of the distinction between sensation and perception.
[2] For a history of this distinction, consult *Reid's Works*, note D.
—J. C. M.

the *Psychological*. But, under this, the ground of principle on which these qualities are divided and designated is, again, twofold. There are, in fact, within the psychological, two special points of view; (1.) that of *Sense*, and (2.) that of *Understanding*.

1. The point of view chronologically prior, or first to us, is that of *Sense*. The principle of division is here the different circumstances under which the qualities are originally and immediately *apprehended*. On this ground, as apprehensions or immediate cognitions through Sense, the *Primary* are distinguished as *objective*, not subjective, as *percepts proper*, not sensations proper; the *Secundo-primary*, as *objective and subjective*, as *percepts proper and sensations proper;* the *Secondary*, as *subjective*, not objective, cognitions, as *sensations proper*, not percepts proper.

2. The other point of view, chronologically posterior, but first in nature, is that of *Understanding.* The principle of division is here the different character under which the qualities, already apprehended, are *conceived* or construed to the mind in thought. On this ground, the *Primary*, being thought as *essential* to the notion of Body, are distinguished from the *Secundo-primary* and *Secondary*, as *accidental;* while the *Primary* and *Secundo-primary,* being thought as *manifest or conceivable in their own nature,* are distinguished from the *Secondary*, as *in their own nature occult and inconceivable.* For the notion of Matter having been once acquired, by reference to that notion, the Primary Qualities are recognized as its *à priori* or necessary constituents; and we clearly conceive how they must exist in bodies in knowing what they are

objectively in themselves ; the Secundo-primary Qualities, again, are recognized as *à posteriori* or contingent modifications of the Primary, and we clearly conceive how they do exist in bodies in knowing what
they are objectively in their conditions ; finally, the
Secondary Qualities are recognized as *à posteriori* or
contingent accidents of matter, but we obscurely surmise how they may exist in bodies only as knowing
what they are subjectively in their effects.

It is thus apparent that the Primary Qualities may
be *deduced à priori*, the bare notion of matter being
given ; they being, in fact, only evolutions of the conditions which that notion necessarily implies ; whereas
the Secundo-primary and Secondary must be *induced
à posteriori;* both being attributes contingently superadded to the naked notion of matter. The Primary
Qualities thus fall more under the point of view of
Understanding, the Secundo-primary and Secondary
more under the point of view of Sense.

I. *Deduction of the Primary Qualities.* —Space or
extension is a necessary form of thought. We cannot
think it as non-existent ; we cannot but think it as
existent. But we are not so necessitated to imagine
the reality of aught occupying space ; for while unable
to conceive as null the space in which the material
universe exists, the material universe itself we can,
without difficulty, annihilate in thought. All that exists in, all that occupies, space, becomes, therefore,
known to us by experience ; we acquire, we con-
struct, its notion. The notion of space is thus native,
or *à priori;* the notion of what space contains, ad-

ventitious, or *à posteriori*. Of this latter class is that of Body or Matter.

Now, we ask, what·are the necessary or essential, in contrast to the contingent or accidental, properties of Body, as apprehended and conceived by us? The answer to this question affords the class of Primary, as contradistinguished from the two classes of Secundo-primary and Secondary Qualities.

It will be admitted that we are able to conceive body only as that which (1.) *occupies space*, and (2.) *is contained in space*. But these catholic conditions of body, though really simple, are logically complex. We may view them in different aspects or relations.

1. The property of *filling space* (Solidity in its unexclusive signification, *Solidity Simple*) implies two correlative conditions: (*a*) the *necessity of trinal extension, in length, breadth, and thickness (Solidity Geometrical); (b)* the corresponding *impossibility of being reduced from what is to what is not thus extended (Solidity Physical, Impenetrability.)*

(*a*) Out of the absolute attribute of *trinal extension* may be again explicated three attributes under the form of necessary relations: (i.) *Number* or *Divisibility;* (ii.) *Size, Bulk,* or *Magnitude;* (iii.) *Shape* or *Figure.*

i. Body necessarily exists, and is necessarily known, either as one body or as many bodies. *Number*, i.e., the alternative attribution of unity or pluralty, is thus, in a first respect, a primary attribute of matter. But, again, every single body is also, in different points of view, at the same time one and many. Considered as a *whole*, it is, and is appre-

hended as actually one; considered as an *extended*
whole, it is, and is conceived, potentially many.
Body being thus necessarily known, if not as already
divided, still as always capable of division, *Divisibility* or *Number* is thus likewise, in a second respect, a
primary attribute of matter.

ii. Body (*multo majus*, this or that body) is not
infinitely extended. Each body must, therefore, have
a certain finite extension, which, by comparison with
that of other bodies, must be less or greater or equal;
in other words, it must by relation have a certain
Size, *Bulk*, or *Magnitude;* and this again, as esti-
mated both (*a*) by the quantity of space occupied
and (*β*) by the quantity of matter occupying, affords
likewise the relative attributes of *Dense* and *Rare*.

iii. Finally, bodies, as not infinitely extended,
have consequently their extension bounded. But
bounded extension is necessarily of a certain *Shape* or
Figure.

(*b*) The negative notion, the impossibility of conceiving the compression of body from an extended to
an unextended, its elimination from space, affords the
positive notion of an insuperable power in body of
resisting such compression or elimination. This
force, which, as absolute, is a conception of the understanding, not an apprehension through sense, has
received no precise or unambiguous name. We might
call it *Ultimate* or *Absolute Incompressibility*.

2. The other most general attribute of matter, that
of *being contained in space*, in like manner affords, by
explication, an absolute and a relative attribute : (*a*)
the *Mobility*, that is, the possible motion, and conse-

quently the possible rest, of a body; and (*b*) the
Situation, Position, Ubication, that is, the local correlation of bodies in space. For

(*a*) Space being conceived as infinite (or rather
being inconceivable as not infinite), and the place occupied by body as finite, body in general, and of
course each body in particular, is conceived capable
either of remaining in the place it now holds, or of
being translated from that to any then unoccupied
part of space. And

(*b*) As every part of space, i.e., every potential
place, holds a certain position relative to every other,
so, consequently, must bodies, in so far as they are
all contained in space, and as each occupies at one
time one determinate space.

II. *Induction of the Secundo-Primary Qualities.*
These qualities are modifications, but contingent modifications, of the primary. They suppose the primary; the primary do not suppose them. They have
all relation to space, and motion in space; and are
all contained under the category of Resistance or
Pressure. For they are all only various forms of a
relative or superable resistance to displacement,
which, we learn by experience, bodies oppose to other
bodies, and, among these, to our organism moving
through space, — a resistance similar in kind (and
therefore clearly conceived) to that absolute or insuperable resistance, which we are compelled, independently of experience, to think that every part of
matter would oppose to any attempt to deprive it of
its space, by compressing it into an inextended.

In so far, therefore, as they suppose the **Primary,**

which are necessary, while they themselves are only
accidental, they exhibit, on the one side, what may
be called a quasi-primary quality; and, in this respect they are to be recognized as percepts, not sensations, as objective affections of things, and not as
subjective affections of us. But, on the other side,
this objective element is always found accompanied
by a Secondary quality or sensorial passion. The
Secundo-primary qualities have thus always two
phases, both immediately apprehended. On their
primary or objective phasis, they manifest themselves
as *degrees* of resistance opposed to our locomotive energy; on their secondary or subjective phasis, as
modes of resistance or pressure affecting our sentient
organism. Thus standing between, and, in a certain
sort, made up of, the two classes of Primary and Secondary qualities, to neither of which, however, can
they be reduced; this their partly common, partly
peculiar nature, vindicates to them the dignity of a
class apart from both the others, and this under the
appropriate appellation of the Secundo-primary Qualities.

They admit of a classification from two different
points of view. They may be (1.) *physically*, they
may be (2.) *psychologically*, distributed.

1. Considered *physically*, or in an objective relation, they are to be reduced to classes corresponding
to the different sources in external nature from which
the resistance or pressure springs. And these sources
are, in all, three: (*a*) that of *Co-attraction;* (*b*)
that of *Repulsion;* (c) that of *Inertia.*

(*a*) Of the resistance of Co-attraction there may

be distinguished, on the same objective principle, two subaltern genera: (i.) that of *Gravity*, or the co-attraction of the particles of body in general; and (ii.) that of *Cohesion*, or the co-attraction of the particles of this and that body in particular.

i. The resistance of Gravity or Weight, according to its degree (which, again, is in proportion to the Bulk and Density of ponderable matter), affords, under it, the relative qualities of *Heavy* and *Light* (absolute and specific).

ii. The resistance of Cohesion (using that term in its most unexclusive universality) contains many species and counter-species. Without proposing an exhaustive, or accurately subordinated, list, of these there may be enumerated (*a*) the *Hard* and *Soft*; (*β*) the *Firm* (Fixed, Stable, Concrete, Solid,) and *Fluid* (Liquid), the Fluid being again subdivided into the *Thick* and *Thin*; (*γ*) the *Viscid* and *Friable*; with (*δ*) the *Tough* and *Brittle* (Ruptile and Irruptile); (*ε*) the *Rigid* and *Flexible*; (*σ*) the *Fissile* and *Infissile*; (*ς*) the *Ductile* and *Inductile* (Extensible and Inextensible); (*η*) the *Retractile* and *Irretractile* (Elastic and Inelastic); (*θ*) (combined with Figure) the *Rough* and *Smooth*; (*ι*) the *Slippery* and *Tenacious*.

(*b*) The resistance from *Repulsion* is divided into the counter-qualities of (i.) the (relatively) *Compressible* and *Incompressible* (ii.) the *Resilient* and *Irresilient* (Elastic and Inelastic).

(*c*) The resistance from *Inertia* (combined with Bulk and Cohesion) comprises the counter-qualities of the (relatively) *Movable* and *Immovable*.

There are thus at least fifteen pairs of counterat-

tributes which we may refer to the secundo-primary
qualities of body; — all obtained by the division and
subdivision of the resisting forces of matter, considered in an objective or physical point of view.

2. Considered *psychologically*, or in a subjective
relation; they are to be discriminated, under the genus
of the *Relatively resisting*, (*a*) according to the *degree* in which the resisting force might counteract our
locomotive faculty or muscular force, and (*b*) according to the *mode* in which it might affect our capacity
of feeling or sentient organism. Of these species, the
former would contain under it the gradations of the
quasi-primary quality, the latter the varieties of the
secondary quality — these constituting the two elements of which, in combination, every secundo-primary quality is made up.

III. *Induction of the Secondary Qualities.* — The
secondary, as manifested to us, are not, in propriety,
qualities of body at all. As apprehended, they are
only subjective affections, and belong only to bodies
in so far as these are supposed furnished with the powers capable of specifically determining the various
parts of our nervous apparatus to the peculiar action,
or rather passion, of which they are susceptible ; which
determined action or passion is the quality of which
alone we are immediately cognizant, the external con-
cause of that internal effect remaining to perception
altogether unknown. Thus, the secondary qualities
(and the same is to be said, *mutatis mutandis*, of the
secundo-primary) are, considered subjectively, and
considered objectively, affections or qualities of things
diametrically opposed in nature, —of the organic and

6

inorganic, of the sentient and insentient, of mind and
matter; and though, as mutually correlative, and their
several pairs rarely obtaining in common language
more than a single name, they cannot well be considered, except in conjunction, under the same category or general class: still their essential contrast of
character must be ever carefully borne in mind. And
in speaking of these qualities, as we are here chiefly
concerned with them on their subjective side, I re-
quest it may be observed, that I shall employ the expression *Secondary qualities* to denote those phenomenal affections determined in our sentient organism by
the agency of external bodies, and not, unless when
otherwise stated, the occult powers themselves from
which that agency proceeds.

Of the secondary qualities, in this relation, there
are various kinds; the variety principally depending
on the differences of the different parts of our nervous
apparatus. Such are the proper sensibles, the idio-
pathic affections of our several organs of sense, as
Color, Sound, Flavor, Savor, and Tactual Sensation;
such are the feelings from Heat, Electricity, Galvanism,
etc.; nor need it be added, such are the muscular and
cutaneous sensations which accompany the perception
of the secundo-primary qualities. Such, though less
directly the result of foreign causes, are Titillation,
Sneezing, Horripilation, Shuddering, the feeling of
what is called Setting-the-teeth-on-edge, etc., etc.;
such, in fine, are all the various sensations of bodily
pleasure and pain determined by the action of external
stimuli. (*Reid's Works*, Note D.)

From the above account of the distinction between

TABULAR CLASSIFICATION OF THE QUALITIES OF BODY.

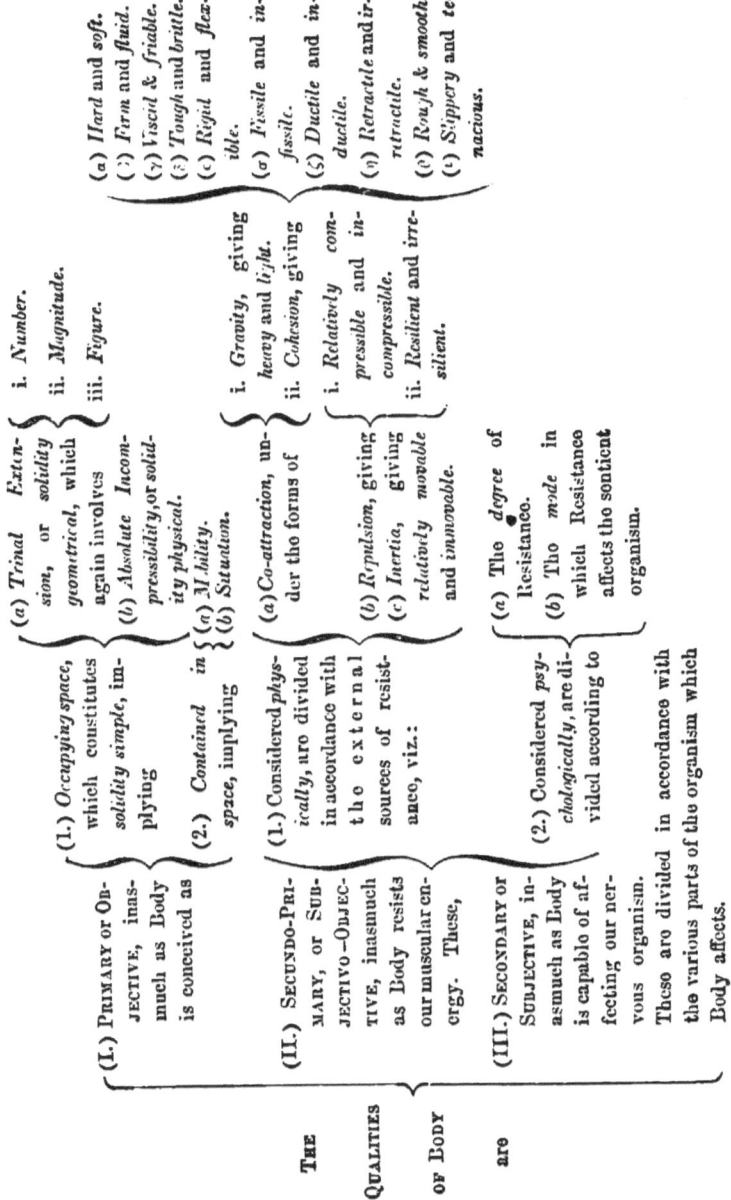

THE QUALITIES OF BODY are —

(I.) PRIMARY OR OBJECTIVE, inasmuch as Body is conceived as

  (1.) Occupying space, which constitutes solidity simple, implying

   (a) Trinal Extension, or solidity geometrical, which again involves
     i. Number.
     ii. Magnitude.
     iii. Figure.

   (b) Absolute Incompressibility, or solidity physical.

  (2.) Contained in space, implying
     (a) Mobility.
     (b) Situation.

(II.) SECUNDO-PRIMARY, or SUBJECTIVO-OBJECTIVE, inasmuch as Body resists our muscular energy. These,

  (1.) Considered physically, are divided in accordance with the external sources of resistance, viz.:

   (a) Co-attraction, under the forms of
     i. Gravity, giving heavy and light.
     ii. Cohesion, giving
       (α) Hard and soft.
       (β) Firm and fluid.
       (γ) Viscid & friable.
       (δ) Tough and brittle.
       (ε) Rigid and flexible.
       (ζ) Fissile and infissile.
       (η) Ductile and inductile.
       (θ) Retractile and irretractile.
       (ι) Rough & smooth.
       (κ) Slippery and tenacious.

   (b) Repulsion, giving
     i. Relatively compressible and incompressible.
     ii. Resilient and irresilient.

   (c) Inertia, giving relatively movable and immovable.

  (2.) Considered psychologically, are divided according to

   (a) The degree of Resistance.

   (b) The mode in which Resistance affects the sentient organism.

(III.) SECONDARY OR SUBJECTIVE, inasmuch as Body is capable of affecting our nervous organism. These are divided in accordance with the various parts of the organism which Body affects.

sensation and perception, and of the distinction in the qualities of matter, it will be seen (1.) that in perception proper the object perceived is always either (*a*) a *primary* quality, or (*b*) the *quasi-primary* phasis of a secundo-primary, (2.) that the primary qualities are perceived as *in our organism*, the *quasi-primary* phasis of the secundo-primary as in correlation to our organism. Thus a perception of the primary qualities does not, originally and in itself, reveal to us the existence, and qualitative existence, of aught beyond the organism, apprehended by us as extended, figured, divided, etc. The primary qualities of things external to our organism we do not perceive, i.e., *immediately know*. For these we only learn to *infer*, from the affections which we come to find that they determine in our organs : — affections which, yielding us a perception of organic extension, we at length discover, by observation and induction, to imply a corresponding extension in the extra-organic agents.

Farther, in no part of the organism have we any apprehension, any immediate knowledge, of extension in its true and absolute magnitude ; perception noting only the fact given in sensation, and sensation affording no standard, by which to measure the dimensions given in one sentient part with those given in another. For, as perceived, extension is only the recognition of one organic affection in its outness from another ; — as a minimum of extension is thus to perception the smallest extent of organism in which sensations can be discriminated as plural ; — and as in one part of the organism the smallest extent is perhaps some million, certainly some myriad, times smaller than in others, —

it follows that, to perception, the same real extension
will appear in this place of the body some million or
myriad times greater than in that. Nor does this
difference subsist only as between sense and sense;
for in the same sense, and even in that sense which
has very commonly been held exclusively to afford a
knowledge of absolute extension, I mean *touch proper*,
the minimum, at one part of the body, is fifty times
greater than it is at another.

The existence of an extra-organic world is apprehended, not in a perception of the primary qualities,
but in a perception of the quasi-primary phasis of the
secundo-primary, that is, in the consciousness that
our locomotive energy is resisted, and not resisted by
aught in our organism itself. For in the consciousness of being thus resisted is involved, as a correlative, the consciousness of a resisting something external to our organism. Both are, therefore, conjunctly
apprehended. This experience presupposes indeed
a possession of the notions of space and motion in
space. But on the doctrine that space, as a necessary
condition, is a native element of thought; and since
the notion of any one of its dimensions, as correlative
to, must inevitably imply, the others, — it is evident
that every perception of sensations out of sensations
will afford the occasion, in apprehending any one, of
conceiving all the three extensions, that is, of conceiving space. On the doctrine, and in the language,
of Reid, our original cognitions of space, motion, etc.,
are instinctive,—a view which is confirmed by the analogy of those of the lower animals which have the
power of locomotion at birth. It is truly an idle

problem to attempt imagining the steps by which we may be supposed to have acquired the notion of exten- sion, when in fact we are unable to imagine to our- selves the possibility of that notion not being always in our possession. We have, therefore, a twofold cog- nition of space ; (1.) an *à priori* or *native* imagination of it, in general, as a necessary condition of the pos- sibility of thought; and (2.) under that, an *à posteriori* or *adventitious* percept of it, in particular, as contingently apprehended in this or that actual complexus of sensations. (*Reid's Works*, pp. 881 –2.)

When, therefore, I concentrate my attention in the simplest act of Perception, I return from my observa- tion with the most irresistible conviction of *two* facts, or rather two branches of the *same* fact, that *I am*, and that *something different from me exists*. In this act, I am conscious of myself as the perceiving *subject*, and of an external reality as the *object* perceived ; and I am conscious of both existences in the same indivi- ible moment of intuition. The knowledge of the sub- ject does not precede or follow the knowledge of the object ; neither determines, neither is determined by, the other. The two terms of correlation stand in mutual counterpoise and equal independence ; they are given as connected in the synthesis of knowledge, but as contrasted in the antithesis of existence.

Such is the fact of Perception revealed in conscious- ness, and as it determines mankind in general in their equal assurance of the reality of an external world, and of the existence of their own minds. Conscious- ness declares our knowledge of material qualities to be intuitive. Nor is the fact, as given, denied even by those who disallow its truth. So clear is the deliverance, that even the philosophers who reject an intuitive perception find it impossible not to admit that their doctrine stands decidedly opposed to the voice of consciousness and the natural conviction of mankind.[1]

The contents of the *fact* of perception, *as given* in consciousness, being thus established, what are the consequences to philosophy, according as the *truth* of its testimony (I.) *is*, or (II.) *is not, admitted?*

(I.) If the veracity of consciousness be unconditionally admitted; if the intuitive knowledge of mind and matter, and the consequent reality of their antithesis be taken as truths, to be explained if possible, but in themselves to be held as paramount to all doubt, —the doctrine is established which we would call the scheme of *Natural Realism*, or *Natural Dualism*.

(II.) But, on the other alternative, five great variations from truth and nature may be conceived; and all of these have actually found their advocates, according as the testimony of consciousness, in the fact of perception (1.), is *wholly*, or (2.) is *partially*, rejected.

1. If *wholly* rejected, that is, if nothing but the phenomenal reality of the fact itself be allowed, the result is *Nihilism*. *).. .. ..*

2. If *partially* rejected, four schemes emerge, according to the way in which the fact is tampered with.

---

[1] For admissions to this effect, see *Reid's Works*, pp. 747-8. — J. C. M.

TABULAR CLASSIFICATION OF THEORIES OF PERCEPTION.

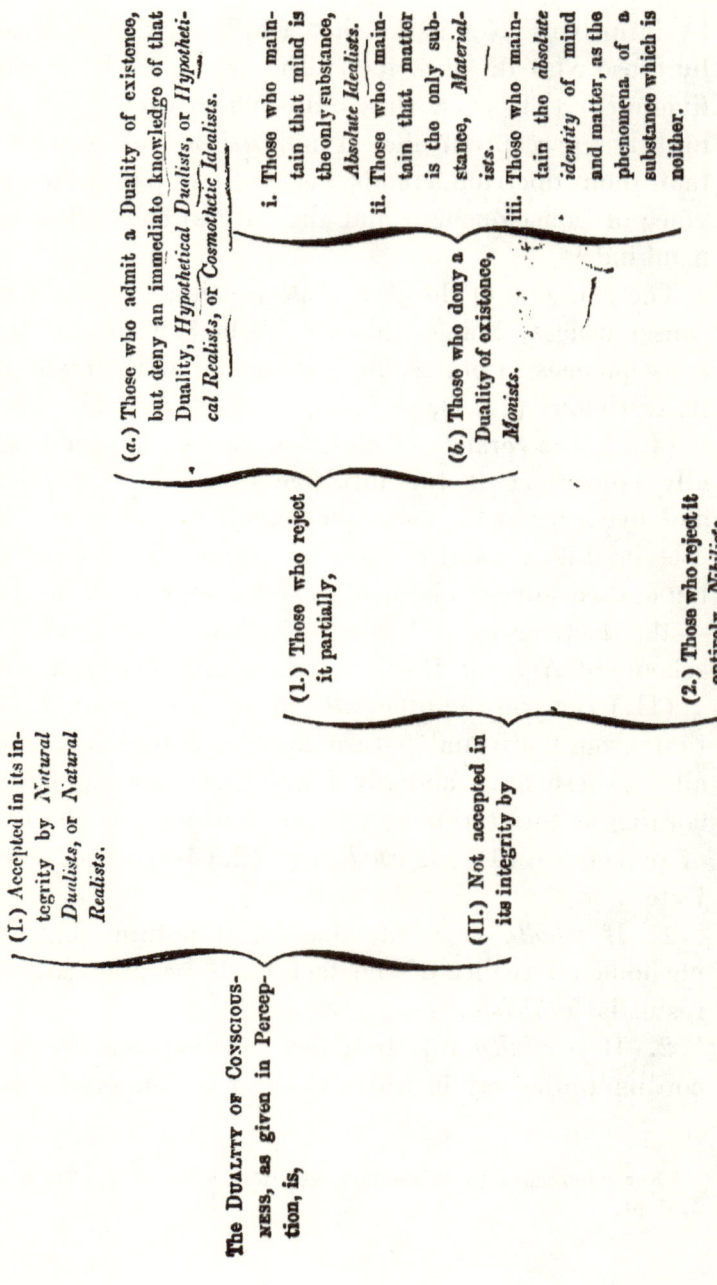

The DUALITY OF CONSCIOUSNESS, as given in Perception, is,

(I.) Accepted in its integrity by *Natural Dualists,* or *Natural Realists.*

(II.) Not accepted in its integrity by

  (1.) Those who reject it partially,

    (*a.*) Those who admit a Duality of existence, but deny an immediate knowledge of that Duality, *Hypothetical Dualists,* or *Hypothetical Realists,* or *Cosmothetic Idealists.*

    (*b.*) Those who deny a Duality of existence, *Monists.*

      i. Those who maintain that mind is the only substance, *Absolute Idealists.*

      ii. Those who maintain that matter is the only substance, *Materialists.*

      iii. Those who maintain the *absolute identity* of mind and matter, as the phenomena of a substance which is neither.

  (2.) Those who reject it entirely, *Nihilists.*

(i.) If the veracity of consciousness be allowed to the equipoise of the object and subject in the act, but rejected as to the reality of their antithesis, the system of *Absolute Identity* emerges, which reduces both mind and matter to phenomenal modifications of the same common substance.

(ii.) and (iii.) If the testimony of consciousness be refused to the co-originality and reciprocal independence of the subject and object, two schemes are determined, according as the one or the other of the terms is placed as the original and genetic. Is the object educed from the subject, *Idealism;* is the subject educed from the object, *Materialism*, is the result.

These systems are all conclusions from an original interpretation of the fact of consciousness in perception, carried intrepidly forth to its legitimate issue. But there is one scheme, which, violating the integrity of this fact, and, with the complete idealist, regarding the object of consciousness in perception as only a modification of the percipient subject, or, at least, a phenomenon numerically different from the object it represents, — endeavors, however, to stop short of the negation of an external world, the reality of which, and the knowledge of whose reality, it seeks by various hypotheses to establish and explain. This scheme, — which we would term *Cosmothetic Idealism,* *Hypothetical Realism,* or *Hypothetical Dualism,* — although the most inconsequent of all systems, has been embraced, under various forms, by the immense majority of philosophers. (*Reid's Works*, pp. 748-9.)[1]

[1] See also *Discussions,* pp. 55-6; and *Lect. on Metaph.* (XVI.) *Reid's Works*, Note C, contain a more elaborate classification of the

§ 2. *SELF-CONSCIOUSNESS.*

This faculty will not occupy us long, as the principal questions regarding its nature and operation have been already considered, in treating of Consciousness in general.

I formerly showed that it is impossible to distinguish Perception, or the other Special Faculties, from Consciousness, — in other words, to reduce Consciousness itself to a special faculty. I stated, however, that though it be incompetent to establish a faculty for the immediate knowledge of the external world, and a faculty for the immediate knowledge of the internal, as two ultimate powers, exclusive of each other, and not merely subordinate forms of a higher immediate knowledge, under which they are comprehended or carried up into one, — I stated, I say, that though the immediate knowledges of matter and of mind are still only modifications of Consciousness, yet that their discrimination, as subaltern faculties, is both allowable and convenient.

The sphere and character of this faculty of acquisition will be best illustrated by contrasting it with the other. Perception is the power by which we are made aware of the phenomena of the external world; Self-consciousness, the power by which we apprehend the phenomena of the internal. The objects of the

various theories of perception. In the *Lect. on Metaph.* (Lect. XXV.) will be found a vindication of Natural Realism; and in the following lecture, a polemic against Hypothetical Realism. — J. C. M.

former are all presented to us in space and time; space and time are thus the two conditions, — the two fundamental forms of external perception. The objects of the latter are all apprehended by us in time and in self; time and self are thus the two conditions, — the two fundamental forms, — of Internal Perception or Self-consciousness. Time is thus a form or condition common to both faculties; while space is a form peculiar to the one, self a form peculiar to the other. What I mean by the *form* or *condition* of a faculty, is that frame, that setting (if I may so speak), out of which no object can be known. Thus, we only know, through Self-consciousness, the phenomena of the Internal world, as modifications of the indivisible Ego or conscious unit; we only know, through perception, the phenomena of the External world, under space, or as modifications of the extended and divisible Non-ego or known plurality. Two difficulties, however, may here be suggested : —

1. It may be asked, if self, or Ego, be the form of Self-consciousness, why is the not-self, the Non-ego, not in like manner called the form of Perception? To this I reply, that the not-self is only a negation, and, though it discriminates the objects of the external cognition from those of the internal, it does not afford to the former any positive bond of union among themselves. This, on the contrary, is supplied to them by the form of Space, out of which they can neither be perceived, nor imagined by the mind. Space, therefore, as the positive condition under which the Non-ego is necessarily known and imagined, and through

which it receives its unity in Consciousness, is properly said to afford the condition, or *form*, of External Perception.

2. But a more important question may be started. If Space, if extension, be a necessary form of thought, this, it may be argued, proves that the mind itself is extended. The reasoning here proceeds upon the assumption that the qualities of the subject knowing must be similar to the qualities of the object known. This, as I have already stated, is a mere philosophical crotchet, — an assumption without a shadow even of probability in its favor. That the mind has the power of perceiving extended objects is no ground for holding that it is itself extended. Still less can it be maintained, that because it has ideally a native or necessary conception of Space, it must really occupy Space. Nothing can be more absurd. On this doctrine, to exist as extended is supposed necessary in order to think extension. But if this analogy hold good, the sphere of *ideal* Space, which the mind can imagine, ought to be limited to the sphere of *real* Space which the mind actually fills. This is not, however, the case; for though the mind be not absolutely unlimited in its power of conceiving Space, still the compass of thought may be viewed as infinite in this respect, as contrasted with the petty point of extension, which the advocates of the doctrine in question allow it to occupy in its corporeal domicile.

The faculty of Self-consciousness affords us a knowledge of the phenomena of our minds. It is the source of Internal experience. You will, therefore, observe,

that, like External Perception, it only furnishes us
with facts; and that the use we make of these facts
— that is, what we find in them, what we deduce
from them — belongs to a different process of intelligence. Self-consciousness affords the materials equally
to all systems of philosophy; all equally admit it, and
all elaborate the materials which this faculty supplies,
according to their fashion. (*Lect. on Metaph.*,
XXIX.)

CHAPTER II.

THE CONSERVATIVE FACULTY.— MEMORY PROPER.

THROUGH the powers of External and Internal Perception, we are enabled to acquire information, — experience; but this acquisition is not of itself independent and complete; it supposes that we are also able to retain knowledge acquired, for we cannot be said to get what we are unable to keep. The faculty of Acquisition is, therefore, only realized through another faculty, — the faculty of Retention or Conservation. Here we have another example of what I have already frequently had occasion to suggest to your observation; we have two faculties, two elementary phenomena, evidently distinct, and yet each depending on the other for its realization. Without a power of Acquisition, a power of Conservation could not be exerted; and, without the latter, the former would be frustrated, for we should lose as fast as we acquired. But as the faculty of Acquisition would be useless without the faculty of Retention, so the faculty of Retention would be useless without the faculties of Re-

94

production and Representation. That the mind retained, beyond the sphere of consciousness, a treasury of knowledge would be of no avail, did it not possess the power of bringing out, and of displaying, — in other words, of reproducing, and representing,— this knowledge in consciousness. But because the faculty of Conservation would be fruitless without the ulterior faculties of Reproduction and Representation, we are not to confound these faculties, or to view the act of mind, which is their joint result, as a simple and elementary phenomenon. Though mutually dependent on each other, the faculties of Conservation, Reproduction, and Representation are governed by different laws, and, in different individuals, are found greatly varying in their comparative vigor. The intimate connection of these three faculties, or elementary activities, is the cause, however, why they have not been distinguished in the analysis of philosophers; and why their distinction is not precisely marked in ordinary language. In ordinary language, we have, indeed, words which, without excluding the other faculties, denote one of these more emphatically. Thus, in the term *Memory*, the Conservative Faculty, the phenomenon of Retention is the central notion, with which, however, those of Reproduction and Representation are associated. In the term *Recollection*, again, the phenomenon of Reproduction is the principal notion, accompanied, however, by those of Retention and Representation, as its subordinates.

By Memory or Retention, you will see, is only meant the condition of Reproduction; and it is, therefore, evident that it is only by an extension of the term that it can be called a faculty, that is, an active power. It is more a passive resistance than an energy, and ought, therefore, perhaps to receive rather the appellation of a capacity. But the nature of this capacity or faculty we must now proceed to consider. (*Lect. on Metaph.*, XXX.)

§ 1. *THE FACT OF RETENTION.*

In the first place, then, I presume that the fact of Retention is admitted. We are conscious of certain cognitions as acquired, and we are conscious of these cognitions as resuscitated. That, in the interval, when out of consciousness, these cognitions do continue to subsist in the mind, is certainly an hypothesis, because whatever is out of consciousness can only be assumed; but it is an hypothesis which we are not only warranted, but necessitated, by the phenomena, to establish. For, besides the phenomena of Retention, there are many which it is impossible to explain by any other hypothesis; and I shall here adduce the evidence which appears to me not merely to warrant, but to necessitate the conclusion, that the sphere of our conscious modifications is only a small circle in the centre of a far wider sphere of action and passion, of which we are only conscious through its effects.

I. *External Perception.* Let us take our first example from Perception, and in that faculty let us commence with

1. *The sense of Sight.* Now, you either already know, or can be at once informed, what it is that has

obtained the name of *Minimum Visibile.* You are of course aware, in general, that vision is the result of the rays of light reflected from the surface of objects to the eye ; a greater number of rays is reflected from a larger surface ; if the superficial extent of an object, and, consequently, the number of rays which it reflects, be diminished beyond a certain limit, the object becomes invisible ; and the *Minimum Visibile* is the smallest expanse which can be seen, — which can consciously affect us, — which we can be conscious of seeing. This being understood, it is plain that, if we divide this *Minimum Visibile* into two parts, neither half can, by itself, be an object of vision, or visual consciousness. They are, severally and apart, to consciousness as zero. But it is evident that each half must, by itself, have produced in us a certain modification, real though unperceived ; for as the perceived whole is nothing but the union of the unperceived halves, so the Perception — the perceived affection itself of which we are conscious — is only the sum of two modifications, each of which severally eludes our consciousness. When we look at a distant forest, we perceive a certain expanse of green. Of this, as an affection of our organism, we are clearly and distinctly conscious. Now, the expanse, of which we are conscious, is evidently made up of parts of which we are not conscious. No leaf, perhaps no tree, may be separately visible. But the greenness of the forest is made up of the greenness of the leaves ; that is, the total impression of which we are conscious is made up of an infinitude of small impressions of which we are not conscious.

7

2. *Sense of Hearing.* — Take another example, from the sense of hearing. In this sense, there is, in like manner, a *Minimum Audibile*, that is, a sound the least which can come into perception and consciousness. But this *Minimum Audibile* is made up of parts which severally affect the sense, but of which affections, separately, we are not conscious, though of their joint result we are. We must, therefore, here likewise admit the reality of modifications beyond the sphere of consciousness. To take a special example. When we hear the distant murmur of the sea, — what are the constituents of the total perception of which we are conscious? This murmur is a sum made up of parts, and the sum would be as zero if the parts did not count as something. The noise of the sea is the complement of the noise of its several waves; — ποντίων τε κυμάτων 'Ανήριθμον γέλασμα — ; and if the noise of each wave made no impression on our sense, the noise of the sea, as the result of these impressions, could not be realized. But the noise of each several wave, at the distance we suppose, is inaudible; we must, however, admit that they produce a certain modification, beyond consciousness, on the percipient subject; for this is necessarily involved in the reality of their result.

3. The same is equally the case in the *other senses;* the taste or smell of a dish, be it agreeable or disagreeable, is composed of a multitude of severally imperceptible effects, which the stimulating particles of the viand cause on different points of the nervous expansion of the gustatory and olfactory organs; and the pleasant or painful feeling of smoothness or rough-

ness is the result of an infinity of unfelt modifications, which the body handled determines on the countless papillæ of the nerves of touch.

II. *Association of Ideas.* — Let us now take an example from another mental process. We have not yet spoken of what is called the Association of Ideas; and it is enough for our present purpose that you should be aware, that one thought suggests another in conformity with certain determinate laws, — laws to which the successions of our whole mental states are subjected. Now, it sometimes happens, that we find one thought rising immediately after another in consciousness, but whose consecution we can reduce to no law of association. In these cases we can generally discover, by an attentive observation, that these two thoughts, though not themselves associated, are each associated with certain other thoughts, so that the whole consecution would have been regular had these intermediate thoughts come into consciousness between the two which are not immediately associated.

You are probably aware of the following fact in mechanics. If a number of billiard balls be placed in a straight row, and touching each other, and if a ball be made to strike, in the line of the row, the ball at one end of the series, what will happen? The motion of the impinging ball is not divided among the whole row; this, which we might *a priori* have expected, does not happen; but the impetus is transmitted through the intermediate balls, which remain each in its place, to the ball at the opposite end of the series, and this ball alone is impelled on. Some-

thing like this seems often to occur in the train of
thought. One idea mediately suggests another into
consciousness, — the suggestion passing through one
or more ideas which do not themselves rise into consciousness. The awakening and awakened ideas here
correspond to the ball striking and the ball struck off;
while the intermediate ideas of which we are unconscious, but which carry on the suggestion, resemble
the intermediate balls which remain moveless, but
communicate the impulse. An instance of this occurs
to me, with which I was recently struck. Thinking
of Ben Lomond, this thought was immediately followed by the thought of the Prussian system of education. Now, conceivable connection between these
two ideas, in themselves, there was none. A little
reflection, however, explained the anomaly. On my
last visit to the mountain, I had met upon its summit
a German gentleman, and though I had no consciousness of the intermediate and unawakened links between
Ben Lomond and the Prussian schools, they were undoubtedly these; the German, — Germany, — Prus-
sia, — and, these media being admitted, the connection between the extremes was manifest.

Mr. Stewart explains this phenomenon on a different hypothesis; but his explanation will be considered
in connection with the similar explanation, which he
gives, of

III. *Our Acquired Habits and Dexterities*, which
in like manner are capable of explanation only on the
theory I have advanced. In these phenomena the
consecution of various operations is extremely rapid;
but it is allowed on all hands that, though we are con-

scious of the series of operations, that is, of the mental state which they conjunctly constitute, — of the several operations themselves as acts of volition we are wholly incognizant. Now, this incognizance may be explained on three possible hypotheses. The *first* regards the whole series of operations as merely mechanical or automatic, and thus denying to the mind all active or voluntary intervention, consequently removes them beyond the sphere of consciousness. The *second*, again, allows to each several motion a separate act of conscious volition ; while the *third*, which I would maintain, holds a medium between these, constitutes the mind the agent, accords to it a conscious volition over the series, but denies to it a consciousness and deliberate volition in regard to each separate movement in the series which it determines.

1. The first of these has been maintained, among others, by two philosophers who in other points are not frequently at one, — by Reid and Hartley. "Habit," says Reid, "differs from instinct, not in its nature, but in its origin ; the last being natural, the first acquired. Both operate without will or intention, without thought, and therefore may be called mechanical principles."

But this opinion is unphilosophical for two reasons. (*a*) In the first place, it assumes an occult, an incomprehensible principle, to enable us to comprehend the effect. (*b*) In the second place, admitting the agency of the mind in accomplishing the series of movements before the habit or dexterity is formed, it afterwards takes it out of the hands of the mind in order to bestow it on another agent. This hypothesis

thus violates the two great laws of philosophizing:
(*a*) to assume no *occult* principle without necessity;
(*b*) to assume no *second* principle without necessity.

2. The second hypothesis, which Mr. Stewart
adopts, is at once complex and contradictory. It
supposes a consciousness and no memory. Now,

(*a*) This is altogether *hypothetical*. It cannot advance a shadow of proof in support of the fact which
it assumes, that an act of consciousness does or can
take place without any, the least, continuance in memory.

(*b*) This assumption is *disproved by the whole analogy of our intellectual nature*. It is a law of mind,
that the intensity of the present consciousness determines the vivacity of the future memory. Memory
and consciousness are thus in the direct ratio of each
other. On the one hand, looking from cause to effect, — vivid consciousness, long memory; faint consciousness, short memory; no consciousness, no
memory; and, on the other, looking from effect to
cause, — long memory, vivid consciousness; short
memory, faint consciousness; no memory, no consciousness. Thus the hypothesis, which postulates
consciousness without memory, violates the fundamental laws of our intellectual being.

(*c*) This hypothesis is at once *illegitimate* and *superfluous*. As we must admit, from the analogy of
perception, that efficient modifications may exist without any consciousness of their existence, and as this
admission affords a solution of the present problem,
the hypothesis in question here again violates the
law of parcimony by assuming, without necessity, a

plurality of principles to account for what one more easily suffices to explain.

3. The third hypothesis, then, — that which employs the single principle of latent agencies to account for so numerous a class of mental phenomena, — how does it explain the phenomenon under consideration? Nothing can be more simple and analogical than its solution. As, — to take an example from vision, — in the external perception of a stationary object, a certain space, an expanse of surface, is necessary to the *minimum visibile;* in other words, an object of sight cannot come into consciousness unless it be of a certain size; in like manner, in the internal perception of a series of mental operations, a certain time, a certain duration, is necessary for the smallest section of continuous energy to which consciousness is competent. Some minimum of time must be admitted as the condition of consciousness, and as time is divisible *ad infinitum,* whatever minimum be taken, there must be admitted to be, beyond the cognizance of consciousness, intervals of time, in which, if mental agencies be performed, these will be latent to consciousness. If we suppose that the minimum of time, to which consciousness can descend, be an interval called six, and that six different movements be performed in this interval, these, it is evident, will appear to consciousness as a simple, indivisible point of modified time; precisely as the *minimum visibile* appears as an indivisible point of modified space. And, as in the extended parts of the *minimum visibile,* each must determine a certain modification on the percipient subject, seeing that the effect of the whole is only the

conjoined effect of its parts, in like manner, the pro-
tended parts of each conscious instant, — of each distinguishable minimum of time, — though themselves
beyond the ken of consciousness, must contribute to
give the character to the whole mental state which
that instant, that minimum, comprises. This being
understood, it is easy to see how we lose the consciousness of the several acts, in the rapid succession
of many of our habits and dexterities. At first,
and before the habit is acquired, every act is slow,
and we are conscious of the effort of deliberation,
choice, and volition ; by degrees, the mind proceeds
with less vacillation and uncertainty ; at length, the
acts become secure and precise : in proportion as this
takes place, the velocity of the procedure is increased,
and as this acceleration rises, the individual acts drop
one by one from consciousness, as we lose the leaves
in retiring further and further from the tree ; and, at
last, we are only aware of the general state which results from these unconscious operations, as we can at
last only perceive the greenness which results from
the unperceived leaves. (*Lect. on Metaph.*, XVIII.
and XIX.)

§ 2. *EXPLANATION OF RETENTION.*

But if it cannot be denied that the knowledge we
have acquired by Perception and Self-consciousness
does actually continue, though out of consciousness,
to endure, can we, in the second place, find any
ground on which to explain the possibility of this en-
durance? I think we can, and shall adduce such an

explanation, founded on the general analogies of our mental nature. The phenomenon of retention is indeed so natural on the ground of the self-energy of mind, that we have no need to suppose any special faculty for memory; the conservation of the action of the mind being involved in the very conception of its power of self-activity.

Let us consider how knowledge is acquired by the mind. Knowledge is not acquired by a mere passive affection, but through the exertion of spontaneous activity on the part of the knowing subject; for though this activity be not exerted without some external excitation, still this excitation is only the occasion on which the mind develops its self-energy. But this energy being once determined, it is natural that it should persist, until again annihilated by other causes. This would, in fact, be the case, were the mind merely passive in the impression it receives; for it is a universal law of nature, that every effect endures as long as it is not modified or opposed by any other effect. But the mental activity, the act of knowledge, of which I now speak, is more than this; it is an energy of the self-active power of a subject one and indivisible; consequently, a part of the Ego must be detached or annihilated, if a cognition once existent be again extinguished. Hence it is, that *the problem most difficult of solution is not, how a mental activity endures, but how it ever vanishes.*

The solution of this problem is to be sought for in the theory of obscure or latent modifications of mind. The disappearance of internal energies from the view of internal perception does not warrant the conclusion that they no longer exist. Every mental activity belongs to the one vital activity of mind in general; it is, therefore, indivisibly bound up with it, and can neither be torn from, nor abolished in, it. But the mind is only capable, at any one moment, of exerting a certain quantity or degree of force. This quantity must, therefore, be divided among the different activities, so that each has only a part; and the sum of force belonging to all the several activities taken together is equal to the quantity or degree of force belonging to the vital activity of mind in general. Thus, in proportion to the greater number of activities in the mind, the less will be the proportion of force which will accrue to each; the feebler, therefore, each will be, and the fainter the vivacity with which it can affect self-consciousness. This weakening of vivacity can, in consequence of the indefinite increase in the number of our mental activities, caused by the ceaseless excitation of the mind to new knowledge, be carried to an indefinite tenuity, without the activities, therefore, ceasing altogether to be. Thus it is quite natural that the great proportion of our mental cognitions should have waxed too feeble to affect our internal perception with the competent intensity; it is quite natural that they should have become obscure or delitescent. In these circumstances, it is to be supposed, that every new cognition, every newly excited activity, should be in the greatest vivacity, and should draw to itself the greatest amount of force; this force will, in the same proportion, be withdrawn from the other earlier cognitions; and it is they, consequently, which must undergo the fate of obscuration.

In further explanation of this faculty I would annex two observations which arise out of the preceding theory.

1. The first is, that retention does not belong alone to the cognitive faculties, but that the same law extends in like manner over all the three primary classes of mental phenomena. It is not cognitions only, but feelings and conations, which are held fast, and which can, therefore, be again awakened. This fact, of the conservation of our practical modifications, is not indeed denied; but psychologists usually so represent the matter, as if, when feelings or conations are retained in the mind, that this takes place only through the medium of the memory; meaning by this, that we must, first of all, have had notions of these affections, which notions being preserved, they, when recalled to mind, do again awaken the modification they represent. From the theory I have detailed to you, it must be seen that there is no need of this intermediation of notions, but that we immediately retain feelings, volitions, and desires, no less than notions and cognitions; inasmuch as all the three classes of fundamental phenomena arise equally out of the vital manifestations of the same one and indivisible subject.

2. The second result of this theory is, that the various attempts to explain memory by physiological hypotheses are as unnecessary as they are untenable. This is not the place to discuss the general problem touching the relation of mind and body. But in prox-

imate reference to memory, it may be satisfactory to
show, that this faculty does not stand in need of such
crude modes of explanation.   It must be allowed, that
no faculty affords a more tempting subject for mate-
rialistic conjecture.   No other mental power betrays
a greater dependence on corporeal conditions than
memory.   Not only, in general, does its vigorous or
feeble activity essentially depend on the health and
indisposition of the body, more especially of the nervous systems; but there is manifested a connection
between certain functions of memory and certain parts
of the cerebral apparatus.   This connection, however,
is such as affords no countenance to any particular
hypotheses at present in vogue.   For example, after
certain diseases, or certain affections of the brain,
some partial loss of memory takes place.   Perhaps
the patient loses the whole of his stock of knowledge
previous to the disease, the faculty of acquiring and
retaining new information remaining entire.   Perhaps
he loses the memory of words, and preserves that of
things.   Perhaps he may retain the memory of nouns,
and lose that of verbs, or *vice versa;* nay, what is
still more marvellous, though it is not a very unfre-
quent occurrence, one language may be taken neatly
out of his retention, without affecting his memory of
others.   By such observations, the older psychologists were led to the various physiological hypotheses
by which they hoped to account for the phenomena
of retention, — as, for example, the hypothesis of permanent material impressions on the brain, — or of
permanent dispositions in the nervous fibres to repeat
the same oscillatory movements, — of particular or-

gans for the different functions of memory, — of particular parts of the brain as the repositories of the various classes of ideas, — or even of a particular fibre as the instrument of every several notion. But all these hypotheses betray only an ignorance of the proper object of philosophy, and of the true nature of the thinking principle. They are at best but useless; for if the unity and self-activity of mind be not denied, it is manifest, that the mental activities, which have been once determined, must persist, and these corporeal explanations are superfluous. (*Lect. on Metaph.*, XXX.)

CHAPTER III.

THE REPRODUCTIVE FACULTY.

I now pass to the next faculty in order, — the faculty which I have called the Reproductive. I am not satisfied with this name; for it does not precisely, of itself, mark what I wish to be expressed, — namely, the process by which what is lying dormant in memory is awakened, as contradistinguished from the representation in consciousness of it as awakened.

Perhaps the *Resuscitative Faculty* would have been better; and the term *Reproduction* might have been employed to comprehend the whole process, made up of the correlative acts of Retention, Resuscitation, and Representation. Be this, however, as it may, I shall at present continue to employ the term in the limited meaning I have already assigned.

Every one is conscious of a ceaseless succession or train of thoughts, one thought suggesting another, which again is the cause of exciting a third, and so on. But if thoughts and feelings and conations (for you must observe, that the train is not limited to the phe-

110

nomena of cognition only) do not arise of themselves, but only in causal connection with preceding and subsequent modifications of mind, it remains to be asked and answered, — Do the links of this chain follow each other under any other condition than that of simple connection? — in other words, *may any thought, feeling, or desire be connected with any other? Or is the succession regulated by other and special laws,* according to which certain kinds of modification exclusively precede, and exclusively follow, each other? The slightest observation of the phenomenon shows that the latter alternative is the case ; and on this all philosophers are agreed. Nor do philosophers differ in regard to what kind of thoughts are associated together. They differ almost exclusively in regard to the subordinate question, of how these thoughts ought to be classified, and carried up into system. This, therefore, is the question to which I shall address myself. (*Lect. on Metaph.*, XXXI.)

The relations, on the ground of which one thought suggests another, give us what may be called the *primary laws of Reproduction;* but when several thoughts are all capable of being suggested by another, as all equally related by the primary laws, what determines which of these thoughts shall actually be suggested? The principles that determine this may be named *secondary laws of Reproduction.*[1]

---

[1] In this paragraph I have attempted an explicit definition of the distinction, as drawn by Hamilton, between the primary and the secondary laws of reproduction. — J. C. M.

§ 1. *PRIMARY LAWS OF REPRODUCTION.*

There are three subjective *unities, wholes,* or *identities,* each of which affords a ground of chronological succession, and reciprocal suggestion, to the several thoughts which they comprehend in one. In other words, Reproduction has *three sources.* These are (1.) The unity of thoughts, differing in *time and modification,* in a co-identity of SUBJECT; (2.) The unity of thoughts, differing in *time,* in a co-identity of MODIFICATION; (3.) The unity of thoughts, differing in *modification,* in a co-identity of TIME. The three unities thus characterized constitute three

(A) GENERAL LAWS OF REPRODUCTION.

I. LAW OF POSSIBLE REPRODUCTION. Of these unities the *first* affords a common principle of the possibility of association, or mutual suggestion for all our mental movements, however different in their character as modifications, however remote in the times of their occurrence; for all, even the most heterogeneous and most distant, are *reproducible, co-suggestible,* or *associable,* as, and only as, phenomena of the same unity of consciousness, — affections of the same indivisible Ego. There thus emerges the LAW OF ASSOCIABILITY OR POSSIBLE CO-SUGGESTION: *All thoughts of the same mental subject are associable, or capable of suggesting one another.*

II. LAWS OF ACTUAL REPRODUCTION. But the unity of subject, the fundamental condition of the associability of thought in general, affords no reason

why this particular thought should, *de facto*, recall or
suggest that. We require, therefore, besides a law
of possible, a law or laws of *actual Reproduction.* Two
such are afforded in the *two* other unities, — those of
Modification and of *Time.*

And now let us, for the sake of subsequent reference, pause a moment to state the following symbolic
illustration : —

$$\text{A B C}$$
$$\text{A}'$$
$$\text{A}''$$

Here the *same letter*, repeated in perpendicular order, is intended to denote the same mental mode,
brought into consciousness, represented, at different
times. Here the *different letters*, in horizontal order,
are supposed to designate the partial thoughts integrant of a total mental state, and therefore coexistent
or *immediately* consequent, at the moment of its actual
realization. This being understood, we proceed : —

Of these two unities that of modification affords the
ground, why, for example, an object determining a
mental modification of a certain complement and character to-day, this presentation tends to call up the
representation of the same modification determined by
that object yesterday. Or suppose, as in our sym-
bols, the three A's to typify the same thought, determined at three different times, be the determining
movement of a presentation or a representation. On
the second occasion, A' will suggest the representation
of A. This it will not be denied that it can do ; for,

8

on the possibility hereof depends the possibility of *simple remembrance.* The total thought, after this suggestion, will be $A' + A$; and on the third occasion, A'' may suggest A' and A; both on this principle, and on that other which we are immediately to consider, of co-identity in time. We have thus, as a first general law of actual Reproduction, Suggestion, or Association : —

1. THE LAW OF REPETITION OR OF DIRECT REMEMBRANCE : *Thoughts, co-identical in modification, but differing in time, tend to suggest each other.*

The unity of *time* affords the ground why thoughts, different in their character as mental modes, but having once been proximately coexistent (including under coexistence immediate consecution) as the parts of some total thought, — and a totality of thought is determined even by a unity of time, — do, when recalled into consciousness, tend immediately to suggest each other, as co-constituents of that former whole, and mediately, that whole itself. Thus let (A, B, C, D, E, F) be supposed a complement of such concomitant thoughts. If A be recalled into consciousness, A will tend to reawaken B, B to reawaken C, and so on, until the whole formerly coexistent series has been reinstated, or the mind diverted by some stronger movement on some other train. We have thus, as a second general law of actual Reproduction, Suggestion, or Association, —

2. THE LAW OF REDINTEGRATION, OF INDIRECT REMEMBRANCE, OR OF REMINISCENCE : *Thoughts, once co-identical in time, are, however different as men-*

tal modes, again suggestive of each other, and that in the mutual order which they originally held.

Philosophers, in generalizing the phenomena of reproduction, have, if the exception of Aristotle be admitted, of these two, exclusively regarded the law of Redintegration. That of Repetition was, however, equally worthy of their consideration. For the excitation of the same by the same, differing in time, is not less marvellous than the excitation of the different by the different, identical in time. It was a principle, too, equally indispensable to explain the phenomena. For the attempts to reduce these to the law of Redintegration alone will not stand the test of criticism; since the reproduction of thought by thought, as disjoined in time, cannot be referred to the reproduction of thought by thought, as conjoined in time. Accordingly we shall find, in coming to detail, that some phenomena are saved by the law of Repetition alone, while others require a combination of the two laws of Repetition and Redintegration. Such combinations of these two laws constitute the

(B) SPECIAL LAWS OF REPRODUCTION. The laws under this head are, —

I. THE LAW OF SIMILARS : *Things, — thoughts, resembling each other (be the resemblance simple or analogical), are mutually suggestive.*

From Aristotle downwards, all who have written on Suggestion, whether intentional or spontaneous, have recognized the association of similar objects. But whilst all have thus fairly acknowledged the effect, none, I think (if Aristotle be not a singular exception), have speculated aright as to the cause.

In general, Similarity has been lightly assumed, lightly laid down, as one of the ultimate principles of associations. Nothing, however, can be clearer than that resembling objects, — resembling mental modifications, — being, *to us*, in their resembling points, *identical*, they must, on the principle of Repetition, call up each other. This, of course, refers principally to suggestion *for the first time*. Subsequently, Redintegration co-operates with Repetition; for *now* the resembling parts have formed together *parts of the same mental whole*, and are, moreover, associated both as *similar* and as *contrasted*.

II. The Law of Contrast: *Things, — thoughts, contrasted with each other (be the contrast one of contrariety or of contradiction), are mutually suggestive.*

1. All contrast is of things contained under a common notion. Qualities are contrasted only as they are similar. A good horse and a bad syllogism have no contrast. Virtue and vice agree as moral attributes; great and little agree as quantities, and as extraordinary deflections from ordinary quantity. Even existence and non-existence are not opposed as different genera, but only as species of existence, — positive existence and negative existence. Conspecies thus (as wolf and dog) may be associated either as similars or as contraries, — similars as opposed to animals of other genera, — contraries as opposed to each other. Contraries are thus united under a higher notion.

2. Affirmation of any quality involves the negation of its contradictory, — the affirmation of goodness is virtually the negation of badness; and many terms

for the contradictory qualities are only negations and affirmations, — just, unjust, — finite, infinite, — partial, impartial.   Hence logical contradictory opposition is even a stronger association than logical contrariety, because only between two.

3. Contrast is a relation, — the knowledge of contraries is one.

4. Consciousness is only of the distinguishable; and therefore contrast most clearly distinguished must heighten consciousness.

III. THE LAW OF CO-ADJACENCY : *Things, — thoughts, related to each other as Cause and Effect, Whole and Parts, Substance and Attribute, Sign and Signified, are mutually suggestive.*

§ 2. SECONDARY LAWS OF REPRODUCTION.

In obedience to the primary laws, movements suggest and are suggested in proportion to the strictness of the dependency between that prior and this posterior.   But such general relation between two thoughts — and on which are founded the two Abstract or Primary laws of Repetition and Redintegration — is frequently crossed, is frequently superseded, by another, and that a particular relation, which determines the suggestion of a movement not warranted by any dependence on its antecedent.   To complete the laws of reproduction we must therefore recognize, as a Secondary or Concrete principle, what may be styled (under protest, for it is hardly deserving of the title Law), THE LAW OF PREFERENCE : *Thoughts are suggested, not merely by force of the general subjective relation subsisting between themselves; they are also suggested in proportion to the relation of interest (from whatever source) in which these stand to the individual mind.*

This general law of Preference yields, as its modes, the special secondary laws; for, under the laws of possibility, one thought being associated with a plurality, and each of that plurality being therefore suggestible, it suggests one in preference to another according to two laws: (1.) By relation to itself, the thought most strictly associated with itself; (2.) By relation to mind, the thought most easily suggestible. That there must be two laws, is shown, because two associated thoughts do not suggest each other with equal force. B may be very strongly associated with A, but A very slightly associated with B. This is twofold; (1.) in order of time, (2.) in order of interest.

(A) Under the *first* head, that of suggestion *by relation to the thought suggesting,* may be stated the following special laws : —

I. THE LAW OF IMMEDIACY : *Of two thoughts, if the one be immediately, the other mediately, connected with a third, the first will be suggested by the third in preference to the second.*

II. THE LAW OF HOMOGENEITY : *A thought will suggest another of the same order in preference to one of a different order.*

Thus a smell will suggest a smell, a sight a sight, an imagination an imagination, in preference to a thought of a different class.

(B) Under the *second* head, that of suggestion *by relation to the mind,* may be stated, as a special law,

THE LAW OF FACILITY: *A thought easier to suggest will be roused in preference to a more difficult one.* The easier are

I. Those *more clearly, strongly impressed* than the reverse. Such are ideas more undistractedly, attentively received; in youth, in the morning; assisted by novelty, wonder, passion, etc. Hence, also, sights are more easily suggested than smells, imaginations than thoughts, etc.

II. Those *more recent*, than older (*cæteris paribus*).

III. Those *more frequently repeated* (*cæteris paribus*).

IV. Those which stand *more isolated from foreign and thwarting thoughts.*

V. Those which are *more connected with homogeneous and assisting thoughts.*

VI. Those more interesting to (1.) natural cognitive powers, talents; (2.) acquired habits of cognition, studies; (3.) temporary line of occupation.

VII. Those more in harmony with affective dispositions, (1.) natural, (2.) habitual, (3.) temporary.[1] (*Reid's Works,* Note D***.)

---

[1] It is due to Sir William Hamilton to bear in mind, that his theory of the laws of reproduction seems never to have been worked into a form perfectly satisfactory to himself. Nearly all that relates to the secondary laws, as well as to the special primary laws, is left in an unfinished state. The exposition in reference to these points, which I have given, is taken, with a few alterations and additions of expression, from the fragments obtained by Mr. Mansel among Sir William's papers. — J. C. M.

§ 3. *DISTINCTION OF SUGGESTION AND-REMINISCENCE.*

The faculty of Reproduction may be considered as operating either spontaneously, without any interference of the will, or as modified in its action by the intervention of volition. In the one case, as in the other, the Reproductive Faculty acts in subservience to its own laws. In the former case, one thought is allowed to suggest another, according to the greater general connection subsisting between them; in the latter, the act of volition, by concentrating attention upon a certain determinate class of associating circumstances, bestows on these circumstances an extraordinary vivacity, and, consequently, enables them to obtain the preponderance, and exclusively to determine the succession of the intellectual train. The former of these cases, where the Reproductive Faculty is left wholly to itself, may not improperly be called Spontaneous Suggestion, or Suggestion simply; the latter ought to obtain the name of Reminiscence or Recollection.

To form a correct notion of the phenomena of Reminiscence, it is requisite that we consider under what conditions it is determined to exertion. In the first place, it is to be noted that, at every crisis of our existence, momentary circumstances are the causes which awaken our activity, and set our recollection at work to supply the necessaries of thought. In the second place, it is as constituting a want (and by *want*, I mean the result either of an act of desire or of volition), that the determining circumstance tends principally to awaken the thoughts with which it is associated. This being the case, we should expect that each circumstance which constitutes a want should suggest, likewise, the notion of an object, or objects, proper to satisfy it; and this is what actually happens. It is, however, further to be observed, that it is not enough that the want suggests the idea of the object; for if that idea were alone, it would remain without effect, since it could not guide me in the procedure I should follow. It is necessary, at the same time, that to the idea of this object there should be associated the notion of the relation of this object to the want, of the place where I may find it, of the means by which I may procure it, and turn it to account, etc. For instance, I wish to make a quotation: this want awakens in me the idea of the author in whom the passage is to be found, which I am desirous of citing; but this idea would be fruitless, unless there were conjoined, at the same time, the representation of the volume, of the place where I may obtain it, of the means I must employ, etc.

Hence I infer, in the first place, that a want does not awaken an idea of its object alone, but that it awakens it accompanied with a number, more or less considerable, of accessory notions, which form, as it were, its train or attendance. This train may vary according to the nature of the want which suggests the notion of an object; but the train can never fall wholly off, and it becomes more indissolubly attached to the object, in proportion as it has been more frequently called up in attendance.

I infer, in the second place, that this accompani-

ment of accessory notions, simultaneously suggested
with the principal idea, is far from being as vividly
and distinctly represented in consciousness as that
idea itself; and when these accessories have once
been completely blended with the habits of the mind,
and its reproductive agency, they at length finally disappear, becoming fused, as it were, in the consciousness of the idea to which they are attached.

Thus, if we appreciate correctly the phenomena of
Reproduction or Reminiscence, we shall recognize, as
an incontestable fact, that our thoughts suggest each
other, not one by one successively, as the order to
which language is astricted might lead us to infer;
but that the complement of circumstances, under which
we at every moment exist, awakens simultaneously
a great number of thoughts; these it calls into the
presence of the mind, either to place them at our disposal, if we find it requisite to employ them, or to
make them co-operate in our deliberations, by giving
them, according to their nature and our habits, an
influence, more or less active, on our judgments and
consequent acts.

It is also to be observed, that, in this great crowd
of thoughts always present to the mind, there is only
a small number of which we are distinctly conscious;
and that, in this small number, we ought to distinguish
those which, being clothed in language oral or mental, become the objects of a more fixed attention;
those which hold a closer relation to circumstances
more impressive than others; or which receive a pre-
dominant character by the more vigorous attention we
bestow on them.   As to the others, although not the

objects of clear consciousness, they are nevertheless present to the mind, there to perform a very important part as motive principles of determination : and the influence which they exert in this capacity is even the more powerful in proportion as it is less apparent, being more disguised by habit. (*Lect. on Metaph.*, XXXII.)

CHAPTER IV.

THE REPRESENTATIVE FACULTY.

By the faculty of Representation, as I formerly mentioned, I mean strictly the power the mind has of holding up vividly before itself the thoughts which, by the act of Reproduction, it has recalled into consciousness. Though the processes of Representation and Reproduction cannot exist independently of each other, they are nevertheless not more to be confounded into one than those of Reproduction and Conservation. They are, indeed, discriminated by differences sufficiently decisive. Reproduction, as we have seen, operates, in part at least, out of consciousness. Representation, on the contrary, is only realized as it is realized in consciousness; the degree or vivacity of the Representation being always in proportion to the degree or vivacity of our consciousness of its reality. Nor are the energies of Representation and Reproduction always exerted by the same individual in equal intensity, any more than the energies of Reproduction and Retention. Some minds are distinguished for a higher

124

power of manifesting one of these phenomena ; others, for manifesting another ; and as it is not always the person who forgets nothing who can most promptly recall what he retains, so neither is it always the person who recollects most easily and correctly who can exhibit what he remembers in the most vivid colors It is to be recollected, however, that Retention, Re-production, and Representation, though not in differ-ent persons of the same relative vigor, are, however, in the same individuals, all strong or weak in refer-ence to the same classes of objects. For example, if a man's memory be more peculiarly retentive of words, his verbal reminiscence and imagination will, in like manner, be more particularly energetic.

In common language, it is not of course to be ex-pected that there should be found terms to express the result of an analysis which had not even been per-formed by philosophers ; and, accordingly, the term *Imagination*, or *Phantasy*, which denotes most nearly the Representative process, does this, how-ever, not without an admixture of other processes, which it is of consequence for scientific precision that we should consider apart.

In the view I take of the fundamental processes, the act of Representation is merely the energy of the mind in holding up to its own contemplation what it is determined to represent. I distinguish, as essen-tially different, the Representation and the determi-nation to represent. I exclude from the Faculty of Representation all power of preference among the ob-jects it holds up to view. This is the function of faculties wholly different from that of Representation, which, though active in representing, is wholly passive as to what it represents. What, then, it may be asked, are the powers by which the Representative Faculty is determined to represent, and to represent this particular object, or this particular complement of objects, and not any other? These are two.

1. The *first* of these is the Reproductive Faculty. This faculty is the great immediate source from which the Representative receives both the materials and the determination to represent; and the laws by which the Reproductive Faculty is governed govern also the Representative. Accordingly, if there were no other laws in the arrangement and combination of thought than those of association, the Representative Faculty would be determined in its manifestations, and in the character of its manifestations, by the Reproductive Faculty alone; and, on this supposition, Representation could no more be distinguished from Reproduction than Reproduction from Association.

2. But there is *another* elementary process which we have not yet considered: Comparison, or the Faculty of Relations, to which the representative act is likewise subject, and which plays a conspicuous part in determining in what combinations objects are represented. By the process of Comparison, the complex objects, called up by the Reproductive Faculty, undergo various operations. They are separated into parts; they are analyzed into elements; and these parts and elements are again compounded in every various fashion. In all this the Representative Faculty co-operates. It, first of all, exhibits the phenomena so called up by the laws of ordinary associa-

tion. In this it acts as handmaid to the Reproductive Faculty. It then exhibits the phenomena as variously elaborated by the analysis and synthesis of the Comparative Faculty, to which, in like manner, it performs the part of a subsidiary.

This being understood, you will easily perceive that the Imagination of common language — the Productive Imagination of philosophers — is nothing but the Representative process, *plus* the process to which I would give the name of the *Comparative*. In this compound operation, it is true that the Representative act is the most conspicuous, perhaps the most essential, element. For, in the *first* place, it is a condition of the possibility of the act of comparison, that the material on which it operates (that is, the objects reproduced in their natural connections) should be held up to its observation in a clear light, in order that it may take note of their various circumstances of relation; and, in the *second*, that the result of its own elaboration, that is, the new arrangements which it proposes, should be realized in a vivid act of Representation. Thus it is, that, in the view both of the vulgar and of philosophers, the more obtrusive, though really the more subordinate, element in this compound process has been elevated into the principal constituent; whereas, the act of Comparison — the act of separation and reconstruction — has been regarded as identical with the act of Representation.

Thus Imagination, in the common acceptation of the term, is not a simple but a compound faculty, — a faculty, however, in which Representation forms the principal constituent. If, therefore, we were obliged

to find a common word for every elementary process
of our analysis, *Imagination* would be the term which,
with the least violence to its meaning, could be accommodated to express the Representative Faculty.

By Imagination, thus limited, you are not to suppose that the faculty of representing mere objects of
sense alone is meant. On the contrary, a vigorous
power of Representation is as indispensable a condition of success in the abstract sciences as in the poetical and plastic arts; and it may, accordingly, be
reasonably doubted whether Aristotle or Homer were
possessed of the more powerful Imagination. The
term *Imagination*, however, is less generally applied
to the representations of the Comparative Faculty
considered in the abstract than to the representations
of sensible objects concretely modified by comparison.
The two kinds of imagination are, in fact, not frequently combined. Accordingly, using the term in
this its ordinary extent, that is, in its limitation to
objects of sense, it is finely said by Mr. Hume:
"Nothing is more dangerous to reason than the flights
of imagination, and nothing has been the occasion of
more mistakes among philosophers. Men of bright
fancies may, in this respect, be compared to those
angels whom the Scriptures represent as covering
their eyes with their wings."

DREAMING, SOMNAMBULISM, REVERIE, are so many
effects of imagination determined by association, — at
least, states of mind in which these have a decisive influence.

1. *Dreaming.* If an impression on the sense often
commences a dream, it is by imagination and sugges-

tion that it is developed and accomplished. Dreams
have frequently a degree of vivacity which enables
them to compete with the reality; and if the events
which they represent to us were in accordance with
the circumstances of time and place in which we stand,
it would be almost impossible to distinguish a vivid
dream from a sensible perception. " If," says Pascal,
" we dreamt every night the same thing, it would perhaps affect us as powerfully as the objects which we
perceive every day. And if an artisan were certain
of dreaming every night for twelve hours that he was
a king, I am convinced that he would be almost as
happy as a king who dreamt for twelve hours that
he was an artisan. . . . . . It is only because
dreams are different and inconsistent, that we can say,
when we awake, that we have dreamt; for life is a
dream a little less inconstant."

The influence of dreams upon our character is not
without its interest. A particular tendency may be
strengthened in a man solely by the repeated action
of dreams. Dreams do not, however, as is commonly
supposed, afford any appreciable indication of the
character of individuals. It is not always the subjects
that occupy us most when awake that form the matter of our dreams; and it is curious that the persons
the dearest to us are precisely those about whom we
dream most rarely.

2. *Somnambulism* is a phenomenon still more astonishing. In this singular state, a person performs
a regular series of rational actions, and those frequently of the most difficult and delicate nature, and,
what is still more marvellous, with a talent to which

9

he could make no pretension when awake. His memory and reminiscence supply him with recollections of words and things which perhaps were never at his disposal in the ordinary state; he speaks more fluently a more refined language; and, if we are to credit what the evidence on which it rests hardly allows us to disbelieve, he has not only perceptions through other channels than the common organs of sense, but the sphere of his cognitions is amplified to an extent far beyond the limits to which sensible perception is confined. This subject is one of the most perplexing in the whole compass of philosophy; for, on the one hand, the phenomena are so marvellous that they cannot be believed, and yet, on the other, they are of so unambiguous and palpable a character, and the witnesses to their reality are so numerous, so intelligent, and so high above every suspicion of deceit, that it is equally impossible to deny credit to what is attested by such ample and unexceptionable evidence.

3. *Reverie.* The third state, that of Reverie, or castle-building, is a kind of waking dream, and does not differ from dreaming, except by the consciousness which accompanies it. In this state, the mind abandons itself without a choice of subject, without control over the mental train, to the involuntary associations of imagination. It is thus occupied without being properly active; it is active, at least, without effort. Young persons, women, the old, the unemployed, and the idle, are all disposed to reverie. There is a pleasure attached to its illusions, which renders it as seductive as it is dangerous. The mind,

by indulgence in this dissipation, becomes enervated ; it acquires the habit of a pleasing idleness, loses its activity, and at length even the power and the desire of action.

ORGANS OF IMAGINATION. I shall terminate the consideration of Imagination Proper by a speculation concerning the organ which it employs in the representations of sensible objects. The organ which it thus employs seems to be no other than the organs themselves of Sense, on which the original impressions were made, and through which they were originally perceived. Experience has shown that Imagination depends on no one part of the cerebral apparatus exclusively. There is no portion of the brain which has not been destroyed by mollification, or induration, or external lesion, without the general faculty of Representation being injured. But experience equally proves that the intracranial portion of any external organ of sense cannot be destroyed without a certain partial abolition of the Imagination Proper. For example, there are many cases recorded by medical observers, of persons losing their sight, who have also lost the faculty of representing the images of visible objects. They no longer call up such objects by reminiscence ; they no longer dream of them. Now, in these cases, it is found that not merely the external instrument of sight — the eye — has been disorganized, but that the disorganization has extended to those parts of the brain which constitute the internal instrument of this sense, that is, the optic nerves and thalami. If the latter — the real organ of vision — remain sound, the eye alone being destroyed, the im-

agination of colors and forms remains as vigorous as
when vision was entire.   Similar cases are recorded
in regard to the deaf.   These facts, added to the observation of the internal phenomena which take place
during our acts of representation, make it, I think,
more than probable that there are as many organs of
Imagination as there are organs of Sense.   Thus I
have a distinct consciousness, that, in the internal
representation of visible objects, the same organs are
at work which operate in the External Perception of
these ; and the same holds good in an imagination of
the objects of Hearing, Touch, Taste, and Smell.

But not only sensible perceptions, voluntary mo-
tions, likewise, are imitated in and by the imagination.
I can, in imagination, represent the action of speech,
the play of the muscles of the countenance, the movement of the limbs ; and when I do this, I feel clearly
that I awaken a kind of tension in the same nerves
through which, by an act of will, I can determine an
overt and voluntary motion of the muscles ; nay,
when the play of imagination is very lively, this external movement is actually determined.   Thus we
frequently see the countenances of persons, under the
influence of imagination, undergo various changes ;
they gesticulate with their hands, they talk to themselves, and all this is in consequence only of the imagined activity going out into real activity.   I should,
therefore, be disposed to conclude, that, as in Perception, the living organs of sense are from without determined to energy, so, in Imagination, they are determined to a similar energy by an influence from
within. (*Lect. on Metaph.*, XXXIII.)

CHAPTER V.

THE ELABORATIVE FACULTY.

THE faculties with which we have been hitherto engaged may be regarded as subsidiary to that which we are now about to consider. This, to which I gave the name of the Elaborative Faculty, the Faculty of Relations, or Comparison, constitutes what is properly denominated Thought, and corresponds to what the Greek philosophers understood by διάνοια, the Latin by Discursus. It supposes always at least two terms, and its act results in a judgment, that is, an affirmation or negation of one of these terms of the other.

In opposition to the views hitherto promulgated in regard to Comparison, I will show that this faculty is at work in every, the simplest, act of mind; and that from the primary affirmation of existence in an original act of consciousness to the judgment contained in the conclusion of an act of reasoning, every operation is only an evolution of the same elementary process, —that there is a difference in the complexity, none in the nature of the act. What I have, therefore, to

133

prove is, in the *first* place, that Comparison is supposed in every, the simplest, act of knowledge; in the *second*, that our factitiously simple, our factitiously complex, our abstract, and our generalized notions are all merely so many products of Comparison; in the *third*, that Judgment, and, in the *fourth*, that Reasoning, is identical with Comparison.

§ 1. *PRIMARY ACTS OF COMPARISON.*

1. The *first* or most elementary act of Comparison, or of that mental process in which the relation of two terms is recognized and affirmed, is the judgment virtually pronounced, in an act of Perception, of the Non-ego, or, in an act of Self-consciousness, of the Ego. This is the primary affirmation of existence. The notion of existence is one native to the mind. It is the primary condition of thought. The first act of experience awoke it, and the first act of consciousness was a subsumption of that of which we were conscious under this notion; in other words, the first act of consciousness was an affirmation of the existence of something. The first or simplest act of Comparison is thus the discrimination of existence from non-existence; and the first or simplest judgment is the affirmation of existence, in other words, the denial of non-existence.

2. But the something of which we are conscious, and of which we predicate existence, in the primary judgment, is twofold, — the Ego and the Non-ego. We are conscious of both, and affirm existence of both. But we do more; we do not merely affirm the

existence of each out of relation to the other, but, in affirming their existence, we affirm their existence in duality, in difference, in mutual contrast; that is, we not only affirm the Ego to exist, but deny it existing as the Non-ego; we not only affirm the Non-ego to exist, but deny it existing as the Ego. The second act of Comparison is thus the discrimination of the Ego and the Non-ego; and the second judgment is the affirmation that each is not the other.

3. The *third* gradation in the act of Comparison is in the recognition of the multiplicity of the coexistent or successive phenomena, presented either to Perception or Self-consciousness, and the judgment in regard to their resemblance or dissimilarity.

4. The *fourth* is the Comparison of the phenomena with the native notion of Substance, and the judgment is the grouping of these phenomena into different bundles, as the attributes of different subjects. In the external world this relation constitutes the distinction of things; in the internal, the distinction of powers.

5. The *fifth* act of Comparison is the collation of successive phenomena under the native notion of Causality, and the affirmation or negation of their mutual relation as cause and effect.

§ 2. CLASSIFICATION.

So far, the process of Comparison is determined merely by objective conditions; hitherto, it has followed only in the footsteps of nature. In those, again, we are now to consider, the procedure is, in a certain sort, artificial, and determined by the necessities of the thinking subject itself. The mind is finite in its powers of comprehension; the objects, on the contrary, which are presented to it, are, in proportion to its limited capacities, infinite in number. How, then, is this disproportion to be equalized? How can the infinity of nature be brought down to the finitude of man? This is done by means of Classification. Objects, though infinite in number, are not infinite in variety; they are all, in a certain sort, repetitions of the same common qualities, and the mind, though lost in the multitude of individuals, can easily grasp the classes into which their resembling attributes enable us to assort them. This whole process of Classification is a mere act of Comparison, as the following deduction will show.

(A) COLLECTIVE NOTIONS. In the first place, this may be shown in regard to the formation of complex notions, with which, as the simplest species of classification, we may commence. By Complex or Collective notions I mean merely the notion of a class formed by the repetition of the same constituent notion. Such are the notions of *an army*, *a forest*, *a town*, *a number*. These are the names of classes, formed by the repetition of the notion of *a soldier*, of *a tree*, of *a house*, of *a unit*. You are not to confound, as has sometimes been done, the notion of *an army*, *a forest*, *a town*, *a number*, with the notions of *army*, *forest*, *town*, and *number;* the former, as I have said, are complex or collective, the latter are general or universal notions.

It is evident that a collective notion is the result of

comparison. The repetition of the same constituent notion supposes that these notions were compared, their identity or absolute similarity affirmed.

In the whole process of classification the mind is in a great measure dependent upon language for its success; and in this, the simplest of the acts of Classification, it may be proper to show how language affords to mind the assistance it requires. Our complex notions being formed by the repetition of the same notion, it is evident that the difficulty we can experience in forming an adequate conception of a class of identical constituents will be determined by the difficulty we have in conceiving a multitude. The comprehension of the mind is limited; it can embrace at once but a small number of objects. It would thus seem that an obstacle is raised to the extension of our complex ideas at the very outset of our combinations. How, then, does the mind proceed? When, by a first combination, we have obtained a complement of notions as complex as the mind can embrace, we give this complement a name. This being done, we regard the assemblage of units thus bound up under a collective name as itself a unit, and proceed, by a second combination, to accumulate these into a new complement of the same extent. To this new complement we give another name; and then again proceed to perform, on this more complex unit, the same operation we had performed on the first; and so we may go on rising from complement to complement to an indefinite extent. Thus, a merchant, having received a large unknown sum of money in crowns, counts out the pieces by fives, and having done this till he has reached twenty, he lays them together in a heap; around these he assembles similar piles of coin, till they amount, let us say, to twenty; and he then puts the whole four hundred into a bag. In this manner he proceeds, until he fills a number of bags, and placing the whole in his coffers, he will have a complex or collective notion of the quantity of crowns which he has received. It is on this principle that arithmetic proceeds; tens, hundreds, thousands, myriads, hundreds of thousands, millions, etc., are all so many factitious units, which enable us to form notions, vague indeed, of what otherwise we could have obtained no conception at all. So much for complex or collective notions, formed without decomposition, — a process which I now go on to consider.

(B) ABSTRACTION. Our thought, that is, the sum total of the Perceptions and Representations which occupy us at any given moment, is always, as I have frequently observed, compound. The composite objects of thoughts may be decomposed in two ways, and for the sake of two different interests.

1. In the first place, we may decompose in order that we may recombine, influenced by the mere pleasure which this plastic operation affords us. This is poetical analysis and synthesis. On this process it is needless to dwell. It is evidently the work of comparison. For example, the minotaur, or chimæra, or centaur, or gryphon (hippogryph), or any other poetical combination of different animals, could only have been effected by an act in which the representations of these animals were compared, and in which certain parts of one were affirmed compatible with

certain parts of another. How, again, is the imagination of all ideal beauty or perfection formed? Simply by comparing the various beauties or excellences of which we have had actual experience, and thus being enabled to pronounce in regard to their common and essential quality.

2. In the second place, we may decompose in the interest of science ; and as the poetical composition was principally accomplished by a separation of integral parts, so this is principally accomplished by an abstraction of constituent qualities. On this process it is necessary to be more particular.

Suppose an unknown body is presented to my senses, and that it is capable of affecting each of these in a certain manner. As furnished with five different organs, each of which serves to introduce a certain class of perceptions and representations into the mind, we naturally distribute all sensible objects into five species of qualities. The abstraction of the senses is thus an operation the most natural ; it is even impossible for us not to perform it. Let us now see whether abstraction by the mind be more arduous than that of the senses.

We have formerly found that the comprehension of the mind is extremely limited : it can only take cognizance of one object at a time, if that be known with full intensity ; and it can accord a simultaneous attention to a very small plurality of objects, and even that imperfectly. Thus it is that attention fixed on one object is tantamount to a withdrawal, to an abstraction, of consciousness from every other. The abstraction of the intellect is thus as natural as that of the senses; it is even imposed by the very constitution of our minds.

But is Abstraction, or rather, is exclusive attention the work of Comparison? This is evident. The application of attention to a particular object, or quality of an object, supposes a choice or preference, and this again supposes Comparison and Judgment. But this may be made more manifest from a view of the act of generalization, on which we are about to enter.

(C) GENERALIZATION. The notion of the figure of the desk before me is an abstract idea, — an idea that makes part of the total notion of that body, and on which I have concentrated my attention, in order to consider it exclusively. This idea is abstract, but it is at the same time individual; it represents the figure of this particular desk, and not the figure of any other body. But had we only individual abstract notions, what would be our knowledge? We should be cognizant only of qualities viewed apart from their subjects (and of separate phenomena there exists none in nature); and as these qualities are also separate from each other, we should have no knowledge of their mutual relations. We should also be overwhelmed with their number.

It is necessary, therefore, that we should form Abstract General notions. This is done when, comparing a number of objects, we seize on their resemblances; when we concentrate our attention on these points of similarity, thus abstracting the mind from a consideration of their differences; and when we give a name to our notion of that circumstance in which they all agree. The General Notion is thus one which makes us know a quality, property, power, action, relation; in short, any point of view under which we recognize a plurality of objects as a unity. It makes us aware of a quality, a point of view, common to many things. It is a notion of resemblance; hence the reason why general names or terms, the signs of general notions, have been called *terms of resemblance* (*termini similitudinis*). In this process of Generalization we do not stop short at a first Generalization. By a first Generalization we have obtained a number of classes of resembling individuals. But these classes we can compare together, observe their similarities, abstract from their differences, and bestow on their common circumstance a common name. On these second classes we can again perform the same operation, and thus ascending the scale of general notions, throwing out of view always a greater number of differences, and seizing always on fewer similarities in the formation of our classes, we arrive at length at the limit of our ascent in the notion of *being* or *existence*. Thus placed on the summit of the scale of classes, we descend by a process the reverse of that by which we have ascended; we divide and subdivide the classes, by introducing always more and more characters, and laying always fewer differences aside; the notions become more and more composite, until we at length arrive at the individual.

I may here notice that there is a twofold kind of quantity to be considered in notions. It is evident that in proportion as the class is high it will, in the first place, contain under it a greater number of classes,

and, in the second, will include the smallest complement of attributes. Thus *being* or *existence* contains under it every class; and yet, when we say that
a thing exists, we say the very least of it that is possible. On the other hand, an individual, though it
contain nothing but itself, involves the largest amount
of predication. For example, when I say, This is
Richard, I not only affirm of the subject every class
from existence down to man, but likewise a number
of circumstances proper to Richard as an individual.
Now, the former of these quantities, the external, is
called the *Extension* of a notion; the latter, the internal quantity, is called its *Comprehension* or *Intension*. They are in the inverse ratio of each other:
the greater the Extension, the less the Comprehension; the greater the Comprehension, the less the Extension.

Having given you this necessary information in regard to the nature of Generalization, I proceed to consider one of the most simple, and, at the same time,
one of the most perplexed, problems in philosophy,—
in regard to the object of consciousness, when we employ a general term. In the explanation of the process of Generalization, all philosophers are at one;
the only differences that arise among them relate to
the point, whether we can form an adequate idea of
that which is denoted by an abstract, or abstract and
general term.

Throwing out of account the ancient doctrine of
Realism, which is curious only in an historical point
of view, there are two opinions which still divide philosophers. Some maintain that *every act and every*

object of mind is necessarily singular, and that the name is that alone which can pretend to generality. Others, again, hold that *the mind is capable of forming notions, representations, correspondent in universality to the classes contained under, or expressed by, the general term.* The former is the doctrine of *Nominalism;* the latter, the doctrine of *Conceptualism.*

The Nominalists maintain that every notion, considered in itself, is singular, but becomes, as it were, general, through the intention of the mind to make it represent every resembling notion, or notion of the same class. Take, for example, the term *man.* Here we can call up no notion, no idea, corresponding to the universality of the class or term. This is manifestly impossible. For as *man* involves contradictory attributes, and as contradictions cannot coexist in one representation, an idea or notion adequate to *man* cannot be realized in thought. The class *man* includes individuals, male and female, white and black and copper-colored, tall and short, fat and thin, straight and crooked, whole and mutilated, etc., etc. ; and the notion of the class must, therefore, at once represent all and none of these. It is, therefore, evident, though the absurdity was maintained by Locke, that we cannot accomplish this ; and, this being impossible, we cannot represent to ourselves the class *man* by any equivalent notion or idea. All that we can do is to call up some individual image, and consider it as representing, though inadequately representing, the generality. This we easily do, for as we can call into imagination any individual, so we can make that individual image stand for any or for every other which

it resembles in those essential points which constitute
the identity of the class. This opinion, which, after
Hobbes, has been maintained, among others, by
Berkeley, Hume, Adam Smith, Campbell, and Stewart, appears to me not only true, but self-evident.

A general notion is nothing but the abstract notion
of a circumstance in which a number of individual objects are found to agree, that is, to resemble each
other. Now, resemblance, being a *relation*, cannot
be represented in Imagination.[1] The two *terms*, the
two relative objects, can be severally imaged in the
sensible phantasy, but not the relation itself. This is
the object of the Comparative Faculty, or of Intelligence Proper. To objects so different as the images
of sense and the unpicturable notions of intelligence,
different names ought to be given; and, accordingly,
this has been done wherever a philosophical nomenclature of the slightest pretensions to perfection has
been formed. In the German language, which is now
the richest in metaphysical expressions of any living
tongue, the two kinds of objects are carefully distinguished. In our language, on the contrary, the terms
idea, conception, notion, are used almost as convertible
for either; and the vagueness and confusion which is
thus produced, even within the narrow sphere of speculation to which the want of the distinction also con-
fines us, can be best appreciated by those who are

---

[1] It must be observed that the term *Imagination* is here used for
the representation of sensible objects alone. See above, p. 128. —
J. C. M.

conversant with the philosophy of the different countries.[1]

In connection with general terms, another curious question has likewise divided philosophers. It is this : *Does Language originate in General Appellatives or by Proper Names?* Did mankind, in the formation of language, and do children, in their first application of it, commence with the one kind of words or with the other? The determination of this question — the question of the *Primum Cognitum,* as it was called in the Schools — is not involved in the question of Nominalism. On this question two opposite theories have been advanced. ✓

1. Many illustrious philosophers have maintained *that all terms, as at first employed, are expressive of individual objects, and that these only subsequently obtain a general acceptation.* This opinion I find maintained by Vives, Locke, Rousseau, Condillac, Adam Smith, Steinbart, Tittel, Brown, and others. "There is nothing," says Locke, "more evident than that the ideas of the persons children converse with (to instance in them alone) are like the persons themselves, only particular. The ideas of the nurse and the mother are well framed in their minds ; and, like pictures of them there, represent only those individuals. The names they first gave to them are confined to these individuals ; and the names of *nurse* and *mamma,* the child uses, determine themselves to those persons.

---

[1] In the *Lect. on Metaph.* (Lect. XXXV.) will be found an elaborate critique of the doctrine of Conceptualism, in the form in which it was maintained by Dr. Thomas Brown. — J. C. M.

Afterwards, when time and a larger acquaintance have made them observe that there are a great many other things in the world that in some common agreements of shape and several other qualities resemble their father and mother, and those persons they have been used to, they frame an idea which they find those many particulars do partake in ; and to that they give, with others, the name *man*, for example. And thus they come to have a general name and a general idea." [1]

2. On the other hand, an opposite doctrine is maintained by many profound philosophers. "General terms," says Leibnitz, "serve not only for the perfection of languages, but are even necessary for their essential constitution. For if by particulars be understood things individual, it would be impossible to speak, if there were only proper names, and no appellatives, that is to say, if there were only names for things individual, since, at every moment, we are met by new ones, when we treat of persons, of accidents, and especially of actions, which are those that we describe the most ; but if by particulars be meant the lowest species (*species infimæ*), besides that it is frequently very difficult to determine them, it is manifest that these are already universals, founded on similarity. Now, as the only difference of *species* and *genera* lies in a similarity of greater or less extent, it is natural to note every kind of similarity or agreement, and consequently to employ general terms of every degree ; nay, the most general being less complex with

---

[1] Locke's *Essay on the Human Understanding*, III., 3, 7.

regard to the essences which they comprehend, although more extensive in relation to the things individual to which they apply, are frequently the easiest to form, and are the most useful. It is likewise seen that children, and those who know but little of the language which they attempt to speak, or little of the subject on which they would employ it, make use of general terms, as *thing, plant, animal*, instead of using proper names, of which they are destitute. And it is certain that all *proper* or individual names have been originally *appellative* or general."[1]

3. But I have now to state a third opinion, intermediate between these, which conciliates both, and seems, moreover, to carry a superior probability in its statement. This opinion maintains, that, as our knowledge proceeds from the confused to the distinct, so, in the mouths of children, *language at first expresses neither the precisely general nor the determinately particular, but the vague and confused;* and that, out of this, the universal is elaborated by generification, the particular and singular by specification and individualization.

Though our capacity of attention be very limited in regard to the number of objects on which a faculty can be simultaneously directed, yet these objects may be large or small. We may make, for example, a single object of attention either of a whole man, or of his face, or of his eye, or of the pupil of his eye, or of a speck upon the pupil. To each of these objects there can only be a certain amount of attentive per-

---

[1] *Nouveaux Essais*, Lib. III., cap, 1.

ception applied, and we can concentrate it all on any
one.   In proportion as the object is larger and more
complex, our attention can of course be less applied
to any part of it, and, consequently, our knowledge of
it in detail will be vaguer and more imperfect.   But
having first acquired a comprehensive knowledge of it
as a whole, we can descend to its several parts, consider these both in themselves, and in relation to each
other, and to the whole of which they are constituents,
and thus attain to a complete and articulate knowledge
of the object.   We decompose, and then we recom-
pose.

But in this we always proceed first by decomposition or analysis.   All analysis indeed supposes a fore-
gone composition or synthesis, because we cannot
decompose what is not already composite.   But in
our acquisition of knowledge, the objects are presented to us compounded ; and they obtain a unity only
in the unity of our consciousness.   The unity of consciousness is, as it were, the frame in which objects
are seen.   I say, then, that the first procedure of
mind in the elaboration of its knowledge is always
analytical.   It descends from the whole to the parts,
— from the vague to the definite.   Definitude, that is,
a knowledge of minute differences, is not, as the opposite theory supposes, the first, but the last, term of
our cognitions.   Between two sheep an ordinary spec-
tator can probably apprehend no difference, and if
they were twice presented to him, he would be unable
to discriminate the one from the other.   But a shepherd can distinguish every individual sheep ; and
why?   Because he has descended from the vague

knowledge which we all have of sheep, — from the vague knowledge which makes every sheep, as it were, only a repetition of the same undifferenced unit, — to a definite knowledge of qualities by which each is contrasted from its neighbor. Now, in this example, we apprehend the sheep by marks not less individual than those by which the shepherd discriminates them; but the whole of each sheep being made an object, the marks by which we know it are the same in each and all, and cannot, therefore, afford the principle by which we can discriminate them from each other. Now this is what appears to me to take place with children. .They first know the things and persons presented to them as wholes. But wholes of the same kind, if we do not descend to their parts, afford us no mark by which we can discriminate the one from the other. Children, thus, originally perceiving similar objects — persons, for example — only as wholes, do at first hardly distinguish them. They apprehend first the more obtrusive marks that separate species from species, and, in consequence of the notorious contrast of dress, men from women; but they do not as yet recognize the finer traits that discriminate individual from individual. But, though thus apprehending individuals only by what we now call their specific or their generic qualities, it is not to be supposed that children know them by any abstract general attributes; that is, by attributes formed by comparison and attention. On the other hand, because their knowledge is not general, it is not to be supposed to be particular or individual, if by particular be meant a separation of species from species, and by individual, the separation of individual from individual: for children are at first apt to confound individuals together, not only in name, but in reality.

What I have now said is, I think, sufficient in regard to the nature of Generalization. It is notoriously a mere act of Comparison. We compare objects; we find them similar in certain respects, that is, in certain respects they affect us in the same manner; we consider the qualities in them, that thus affect us in the same manner, as the same; and to this common quality we give a name; and as we can predicate this name of all and each of the resembling objects, it constitutes them into a class. Aristotle has truly said that general names are only abbreviated definitions, and definitions, you know, are judgments. For example, *animal* is only a compendious expression for *organized and animated body; man*, only a summary of *rational animal*, etc.

§ 3. *JUDGMENT.*

In the processes of *judgment* and *reasoning*, the act of Comparison is a judgment of something more than a mere affirmation of the existence of a phenomenon, — something more than a mere discrimination of one phenomenon from another; and, accordingly, while it has happened that the intervention of judgment in every, even the simplest, act of primary cognition, as monotonous and rapid, has been overlooked, the name has been exclusively limited to the more varied and elaborate comparison of one notion with another, and **the enouncement of their agreement or disagreement.**

It is in the discharge of this, its more obtrusive function, that we are now about to consider the Elaborative Faculty.

I have already noticed that our knowledge does not commence with the individual and the most particular objects of knowledge, — that we do not rise in any regular progress from the less to the more general, first considering the qualities which characterize individuals, then those which belong to species and genera, in regular ascent. On the contrary, our knowledge commences with the vague and confused. Out of this the general and the individual are both equally evolved. In consequence of this genealogy of our knowledge we usually commence by bestowing a name upon a whole object or congeries of objects, of which, however, we possess only a partial and indefinite conception. In the sequel, this vague notion becomes somewhat more determinate; the partial idea which we had becomes enlarged by new accessions; by degrees our conception waxes fuller, and represents a greater number of attributes. With this conception, thus amplified and improved, we compare the last notion which has been acquired; that is to say, we compare a part with its whole, or with the other parts of this whole, and, finding that it is harmonious, — that it dovetails and naturally assorts with other parts, — we acquiesce in this union; and this we denominate an act of judgment.

I have the conception of a triangle, and this conception is composed in my mind of several others. Among these partial notions, I select that of two sides greater than the third, and this notion, which I had at first, as it were, taken apart, I reunite with the others from which it had been separated, saying the triangle contains always two sides, which together are greater than the third.

Every time we judge, we compare a total conception with a partial, and we recognize that the latter really constitutes a part of the former. One of these conceptions has received the name of *subject;* the other, that of *attribute* or *predicate.* The verb which connects these two parts is called the *copula.* *The quadrangle is a double triangle; nine is an odd number; body is divisible.* Here *quadrangle, nine, body,* are subjects : *a double triangle, an odd number, divisible,* are predicates. The whole mental judgment, formed by the subject, predicate, and copula, is called, when enounced in words, *proposition.*

In discourse, the parts of a proposition are not always found placed in logical order; but to discover and discriminate them, it is only requisite to ask, *What is the thing of which something else is affirmed or denied?* The answer to this question will point out *the subject;* and we shall find *the predicate* if we inquire, *What is affirmed or denied of the matter of which we speak?*

In fine, when we judge, we must have, in the first place, at least two notions ; in the second place, we compare these ; in the third, we recognize that one contains or excludes the other ; and, in the fourth, we acquiesce in this recognition.

§ 4. *REASONING.*

Simple Comparison or Judgment is conversant with two notions, the one of which is contained in the other. But it often happens that one notion is contained in another not immediately, but mediately, and we may be able to recognize the relation of these to each other only through a third, which, as it immediately contains the one, is immediately contained in the other. Take the notions A, B, C, — A contains B; B contains C; A therefore also contains C. But as, *ex hypothesi*, we do not at once and directly know C as contained in A, we cannot immediately compare them together and judge of their relation. We therefore perform a double or complex process of comparison; we compare B with A, and C with B, and then C with A through B. We say, B is a part of A; C is a part of B; therefore C is a part of A. This double act of comparison has obtained the name of *Reasoning;* the term *Judgment* being left to express the simple act of comparison, or rather its result.

Reasoning is either from the whole to its parts; or from all the parts, discretively, to the whole they constitute, collectively. The former of these is Deductive, the latter is Inductive, Reasoning. The statement you will find, in all logical books, of reasonings from certain parts to the whole, or from certain parts to certain parts, is erroneous. I shall first speak of the reasoning from the whole to its parts, — or of

I. *Deductive Reasoning.* It is self-evident, that *whatever is the part of a part is a part of the whole.*

This one axiom is the foundation of all reasoning from the whole to the parts. There are, however, two kinds of whole and parts; and these constitute two varieties, or rather two phases, of deductive reasoning. This distinction, which is of the most important kind, has nevertheless been wholly overlooked by philosophers, in consequence of which the utmost perplexity and confusion have been introduced into the science.

I have formerly stated that a proposition consists of two terms, — the subject and the predicate. Now, in different relations we may regard the subject as the whole and the predicate as its part, or the predicate as the whole and the subject as its part.

Let us take the proposition, *milk is white*. Now, here we may either consider the predicate *white* as one of a number of attributes, the whole complement of which constitutes the subject *milk*. In this point of view, the predicate is a part of the subject. Or, again, we may consider the predicate *white* as the name of a class of objects, of which the subject is one. In this point of view, the subject is a part of the predicate.

You will remember the distinction, which I formerly stated, of the twofold quantity of notions or terms. The Extension of a notion or term corresponds to the greater number of subjects contained under a predicate; the Intension, or Comprehension, of a notion or term, to the greater number of predicates contained in a subject. These quantities or wholes are always in the inverse ratio of each other. Now, it is singular that logicians should have taken this distinction between notions, and yet not have thought of applying it to reasoning.   But so it is ; and this is not the only oversight they have committed in the application of the very primary principles of their science.   The great distinction we have established between the subject and predicate considered severally, as, in different relations, whole and as part, constitutes the primary and principal division of Syllogisms, both Deductive and Inductive ; and its introduction wipes off a complex mass of rules and qualifications, which the want of it rendered necessary.   I can, of course, at present, only explain in general the nature of this distinction ; its details belong to the science of the Laws of Thought, or Logic, of which we are not here to treat.

1. *Deductive Reasoning in Comprehension.* I shall first consider the process of that Deductive Inference in which the subject is viewed as the whole, the predicate as the part.   In this reasoning, the whole is determined by the Comprehension, and is, again, either a Physical or Essential whole, or an Integral or Mathematical whole.   (*a*) A Physical or Essential whole is that which consists of not really separable parts, of or pertaining to its substance.   Thus, man is made up of two substantial parts, — a mind and a body ; and each of these has again various qualities, which, though separable only by mental abstraction, are considered as so many parts of an essential whole.   Thus the attributes of respiration, of digestion, of locomotion, of color, are so many parts of the whole notion we have of the human body ; cognition, feeling, desire, virtue, vice, etc., so many parts of the whole notion we have of the human mind ; and all these together, so many

parts of the whole notion we have of man. (*b*) A Mathematical or Integral or Quantitative whole is that which has part out of part, and which therefore can be really partitioned. The Integral, or, as it ought to be called, Integrate whole (*totum integratum*) is composed of integrant parts (*partes integrantes*), which are either homogeneous or heterogeneous. An example of the former is given in the division of a square into two triangles; of the latter, in the division of the animal body into head, trunk, extremities, etc.

This being understood, let us consider how we proceed when we reason from the relation between a comprehensive whole and its parts. Here it is evident that all the parts of the predicate must also be parts of the subject; in other terms, all that belongs to the predicate must also belong to the subject. In the words of the scholastic adage, *Nota notæ est nota rei ipsius; Predicatum predicati est predicatum subjecti.* An example of this reasoning : —

Europe contains England ;

England contains Middlesex ;

Therefore, Europe contains Middlesex.

In other words, England is an integrant part of Europe ; Middlesex is an integrant part of Europe. This is an example from a mathematical whole and parts. Again : —

Socrates is just (that is, Socrates contains justice as a quality) ;

Justice is a virtue (that is, justice contains virtue as a constituent part) ;

Therefore, Socrates is virtuous.

In other words, justice is an attribute or essential
part of Socrates; virtue is an attribute or essential
part of justice; therefore, virtue is an attribute or
essential part of Socrates. This is an example from
a physical or essential whole and parts.

2. *Deductive Reasoning in Extension.* I proceed,
in the second place, to the other kind of Deductive
Reasoning, — that in which the subject is the part,
the predicate is the whole. This reasoning proceeds
under that species of whole which has been called the
Logical, or Potential, or Universal. This whole is
determined by the Extension of a notion; the genera
having species, and the species individuals, as their
parts. The parts of a logical or universal whole are
called the *subject parts.*

From what you know of the process of generalization, you are aware that general terms are expressive
of attributes which may be predicated of many different objects; and inasmuch as these objects resemble
each other in the common attribute, they are considered by us as constituting a class. Thus, when I say
that a horse is a quadruped; Bucephalus is a horse;
therefore, Bucephalus is a quadruped; — I virtually
say, — *horse*, the subject, is a part of the predicate
quadruped; Bucephalus, the subject, is part of the
predicate *horse;* therefore, *Bucephalus*, the subject, is
part of the predicate *quadruped.* In the reasoning
under this whole you will observe that the same word,
as it is whole or part, changes from predicate to subject; *horse*, when viewed as a part of *quadruped*, being the subject of the proposition; whereas, when

viewed as a whole containing *Bucephalus*, it becomes the predicate.

II. *Inductive Reasoning* is founded on the principle, that *what is true of every constituent part belongs, or does not belong, to the constituted whole.* Induction, like Deduction, may be divided into two kinds, according as the whole and parts, about which it is conversant, are Comprehensive or Extensive.

1. Thus, in the *former:* —

Gold is a metal, yellow, ductile, fusible in *aqua regia*, of a certain specific gravity, and so on;

These qualities constitute this body (are all its parts);

Therefore, this body is gold.

2. In the *latter:* —

Ox, horse, dog, etc., are animals, that is, are contained under the class animal;

Ox, horse, dog, etc., constitute (are all the constituents of) the class quadruped;

Therefore, quadruped is contained under animal.

Both in the Deductive and Inductive processes the inference must be of an absolute necessity, in so far as the mental illation is concerned; that is, every consequent proposition must be evolved out of every antecedent proposition with intuitive evidence. I do not mean, by this, that the antecedent should be necessarily true, or that the consequent be really contained in it; it is sufficient that the antecedent be assumed as true, and that the consequent be, in conformity to the laws of thought, evolved out of it as its part or its equation. This last is called Logical or Formal or Subjective truth; and an inference may be subjectively or formally true, which is objectively or really false.

The account given of Induction in all works of Logic is utterly erroneous. Sometimes we find this inference described as a precarious, not a necessary, reasoning. It is called an illation from some to all. But here *the some*, as it neither contains nor constitutes *the all*, determines no necessary movement, and a conclusion drawn under these circumstances is logically vicious. Others again describe the Inductive process thus : —

What belongs to some objects of a class belongs to the whole class ;

This property belongs to some objects of the class ;

Therefore, it belongs to the whole class.

This account of Induction, which is the one you will find in all the English works on Logic, is not an inductive reasoning at all. It is, logically considered, a deductive syllogism ; and, logically considered, a syllogism radically vicious. It is logically vicious to say, that, because some individuals of a class have certain common qualities apart from that property which constitutes the class itself, therefore the whole individuals of the class should partake in these qualities. For this there is no logical reason, — no necessity of thought. The probability of this inference, and it is only probable, is founded on the observation of the analogy of nature, and, therefore, not upon the laws of thought by which alone reasoning, considered as a logical process, is exclusively governed. To become a formally legitimate induction, the objective probability must be clothed with a subjective necessity, and *the some* must be translated into *the all* which it is supposed to represent.

In the deductive syllogism we proceed by analysis, that is, by decomposing a whole into its parts; but as the two wholes with which reasoning is conversant are in the inverse ratio of each other, so our analysis in the one will correspond to our synthesis in the other. For example, when I divide a whole of extension into its parts, — when I divide a genus into the species, a species into the individuals it contains, — I do so by adding new differences, and thus go on accumulating in the parts a complement of qualities which did not belong to the wholes. This, therefore, which, in point of extension, is an analysis, is, in point of comprehension, a synthesis. In like manner, when I decompose a whole of comprehension, that is, decompose a complex predicate into its constituent attributes, I obtain by this process a simpler and more general quality, and thus this, which, in relation to a comprehensive whole, is an analysis, is, in relation to an extensive whole, a synthesis. As the deductive inference is Analytic, the inductive is Synthetic. But as induction, equally as deduction, is conversant with both wholes, so the synthesis of induction on the comprehensive whole is a reversed process to its synthesis on the extensive whole.

• You will therefore be aware, that the terms *analysis* and *synthesis*, when used without qualification, may be employed at cross purposes, to denote operations precisely the converse of each other. And so it has happened. Analysis, in the mouth of one set of philosophers, means precisely what synthesis denotes in the mouth of another; nay, what is even still more frequent, these words are perpetually converted with each other by the same philosopher. I may notice, what has rarely, if ever, been remarked, that *synthesis*, in the writings of the Greek logicians, is equivalent to the *analysis* of modern philosophers; the former, regarding the extensive whole as the principal, applied analysis, κατ᾽ ἐξοχήν, to its division; the latter, viewing the comprehensive whole as the principal, in general limit analysis to its decomposition. This, however, has been overlooked, and a confusion the most inextricable prevails in regard to the use of these words, if the thread of the labyrinth is not obtained. (*Lect. on Metaph.*, XXXIV.–XXXVII.)

11

CHAPTER VI.

THE REGULATIVE FACULTY.

I now enter upon the last of the Cognitive Faculties, — the faculty which I denominated the Regulative. Here the term *faculty*, you will observe, is employed in a somewhat peculiar signification, for it is employed not to denote the proximate cause of any definite energy, but the power the mind has of being the native source of certain necessary or *à priori* cognitions; which cognitions, as they are the conditions, the forms, under which our knowledge in general is possible, constitute so many fundamental laws of intellectual nature. It is in this sense that I call the power which the mind possesses of modifying the knowledge it receives, in conformity to its proper nature, its Regulative Faculty. The Regulative Faculty is, however, in fact, nothing more than the complement of such laws; it is the *locus principiorum*. It thus corresponds to what was known in the Greek philosophy under the name of νοῦς, when that term was rigorously used. To this faculty has been latterly applied

162

the name *Reason;* but this term is so vague and ambiguous, that it is almost unfitted to convey any definite meaning. The term *Common Sense* has likewise been applied to designate the place of principles. This word is also ambiguous. In the *first* place, it was the expression used in the Aristotelic philosophy to denote the *Central or Common Sensory, in which the different external senses met and were united.* In the *second* place, it was employed to signify *a sound understanding applied to vulgar objects, in contrast to a scientific or speculative intelligence;* and it is in this signification that it has been taken by those who have derided the principle on which the philosophy, which has been distinctively denominated the Scottish, professes to be established. This is not, however, the meaning which has always, or even principally, been attached to it; and an incomparably stronger case might be made out in defence of this expression than has been done by Reid, or even by Mr. Stewart. It is, in fact, a term of high antiquity and very general acceptation. Were it allowed in metaphysical philosophy, as in physical, to discriminate scientific differences by scientific terms, I would employ the word *noetic,* as derived from νοῦς, to express all those cognitions that originate in the mind itself; *dianoetic* to denote the operations of the Discursive, Elaborative, or Comparative Faculty.[1] (*Lect. on Metaph.,* XXXVIII.)

---

[1] For an account of the various names by which the principles of *Common Sense* have been designated, see *Reid's Works,* Note A. This note is an elaborate dissertation on the *Philosophy of Common Sense,* and deserves study in this connection. — J. C. M.

The essential notes or characters, by which we are enabled to distinguish our original from our derivative cognitions, may be reduced to four : ~~*by reason' validity* ~~

1. Their *Incomprehensibility.* When we are able to comprehend how or why a thing is, the belief of the existence of that thing is not a primary datum of consciousness, but a subsumption under the cognition or belief which affords its reason.

2. Their *Simplicity.* If a cognition or belief be made up of, and can be explicated into, a plurality of cognitions or beliefs, it is manifest that, as compound, it cannot be original.

3. Their *Necessity and Absolute Universality.* These may be regarded as coincident. For when a belief is necessary, it is, *eo ipso,* universal; and that a belief is universal is a certain index that it must be necessary. To prove the necessity, the universality must, however, be absolute; for a relative universality indicates no more than custom and education, howbeit the subjects themselves may deem that they follow the dictates of nature.

4. Their *Comparative Evidence and Certainty.* This, along with the third, is well stated by Aristotle : "What *appears to all,* that we affirm *to be;* and he who rejects this belief will assuredly advance *nothing better deserving of credence.*" (*Reid's Works,* pp. 754–5.)

Though it be now generally acknowledged, by the profoundest thinkers, that it is impossible to analyze all our knowledge into the produce of experience, external or internal, and that a certain complement of cognitions must be allowed as having their origin in the nature of the thinking principle itself; they are not at one in regard to those which ought to be recognized as ultimate and elemental, and those which ought to be regarded as modifications or combinations of these. The reduction of our native cognitions to system is therefore a problem which still remains to be solved. These cognitions are founded on the necessary conditions of thought; and we have now to see that philosophers have failed to enumerate all those conditions. (*Lect. on Metaph.*, XXXVIII.)

Now, the conditions of all positive thought are two: (1.) *Non-contradiction;* (2.) *Relativity*. If either of these conditions be violated, thought (employing that term as comprehending all our cognitive energies) is not *positive,* — it is only *negative;* for thought is positive only when existence, objective or subjective, is predicated of an object. If the condition of Non-contradiction be not fulfilled, there emerges *The really impossible.* — *Nihil purum;* if that of Relativity be not purified, there results *The Impossible to Thought,* — *Nihil cogitabile.* It might be supposed that negative thinking, being a negation of thought, is in propriety a negation therefore, absolutely, of all mental activity. But this would be erroneous. In fact, as Aristotle observes, every negation involves an affirmation, and we cannot think or predicate non-existence except by reference to existence. Thus even negative thought is realized only under the condition of Relativity and positive thinking. For example, we try to think, — to predicate existence in some way, — but find ourselves unable. We then predicate *incogitability;* and if we do not always predicate, as an equivalent, (objective) *non-existence*, we shall never err.

It is only, then, when both of these conditions are fulfilled, that we think — *Something*.

§ 1. *THE CONDITION OF NON-CONTRADICTION.*

This condition is insuperable. We think it not only as a law of thought, but as a law of things ; and while we suppose its violation to determine an absolute impossibility, we suppose its fulfilment to afford only the *Not-impossible*. Thought is, under this condition, merely *explicative* or *analytic;* and the condition itself is brought to bear under three phases, constituting three laws: (1.) the law of *Identity:* (2.) the law of *Contradiction* (more properly Non-contradiction); (3.) the law of *Excluded Middle* (between two contradictories).[1] The science of these is *Logic;* and as the laws are only explicative, Logic is only *formal*.

Though necessary to state the condition of Non-contradiction, there is no dispute about its effect, no danger of its violation. When, therefore, I speak of the *Conditioned*, the term is used in special reference to Relativity. By existence Conditioned is meant emphatically existence relative, — existence thought under relation. Relation may thus be understood to contain all the categories and forms of positive thought. (*Discussions*, pp. 602–3.)

---

[1] For a full discussion of these laws see *Lect. on Log.*, V. and VI. ; and Appendix IV. — J. C. M.

§ 2. *THE CONDITION OF RELATIVITY.*

By this condition it is implied that the mind can conceive, and can consequently know, *only the limited, and the conditionally limited.* The unconditionally unlimited, or the *Infinite*, the unconditionally limited, or the *Absolute*, cannot positively be construed to the mind ; they can be conceived only by a thinking away from, or abstraction of, those very conditions under which thought itself is realized : consequently the notion of the Unconditioned is only negative, — negative of the conceivable itself. For example : —

I. On the one hand, we can positively conceive neither (1.) an *absolute whole*, that is, a whole so great that we cannot also conceive it as a relative part of a still greater whole, nor (2.) an *absolute part*, that is, a part so small that we cannot also conceive it as a relative whole, divisible into smaller parts.

II. On the other hand, we cannot positively represent or realize or construe to the mind (as here Understanding and Imagination coincide), (1.) an *infinite whole*, for this could only be done by the infinite synthesis in thought of finite wholes, which would require an infinite time for its accomplishment ; nor (2.), for the same reason, can we follow out in thought an *infinite divisibility of parts*.

The result is the same whether we apply the process to limitation in *space*, in *time*, or in *degree*. The unconditional negation and the unconditional affirmation of limitation — in other words, the *Infinite* and the *Absolute*, properly so called — are thus equally

inconceivable to us. The conditionally limited (which
we may briefly call the *Conditioned*) is thus the only
possible object of knowledge and of positive thought ;
thought necessarily supposes condition. For as the
eagle cannot outsoar the atmosphere in which he floats,
and by which alone he is supported ; so the mind cannot transcend that sphere of limitation within and
through which exclusively the possibility of thought
is realized.

The Conditioned is the mean between two extremes,
— two inconditionates, exclusive of each other, *neither
of which can be conceived as possible*, but of which, on
the principles of contradiction and excluded middle,
one must be admitted as necessary. Our faculties are
thus shown to be weak, but not deceitful. The mind
is not represented as conceiving two propositions,
subversive of each other, as equally possible ; but
only as unable to understand, as possible, either of
two extremes, one of which, however, on the ground ·
of their mutual repugnance, it is compelled to recognize as true. We are thus taught the salutary lesson,
that the capacity of thought is not to be constituted
into the measure of existence ; and are warned from
recognizing the domain of our knowledge as necessarily coextensive with the horizon of our faith. And,
by a wonderful revelation, we are thus, in the very
consciousness of our inability to conceive aught above
the relative and finite, inspired with a belief in the
existence of something unconditioned beyond the
sphere of all reprehensible reality. (*Discussions*, pp.
13–15.)

The condition of Relativity is therefore not insuperable. We should think it not as a law of things, but merely as a law of thought. Thinking, under this condition, is *ampliative* or *synthetic*. Its science, *Metaphysic*, using that term in a comprehensive meaning, is therefore *material*, in the sense of non-formal.

The relations under which this condition is brought to bear are either *necessary* and *original*, or *contingent* and *derivative*. The latter are such as One and Other, End and Mean, Whole and Part, etc., etc. Relations like these, which we frequently employ in the actual applications of our cognitive energies, admit of classification from different points of view; but to attempt their arrangement at all, far less on any exclusive principle, would here be manifestly out of place. In so far, then, as it is necessary, the condition of Relativity is brought to bear under two principal relations; the one springing from the *subject* of knowledge (*the relation of Knowledge*), the other from the *object* of knowledge (*the relations of Existence*).

(A) THE RELATION OF KNOWLEDGE is that which arises from the reciprocal dependence of the subject and object of thought. Whatever comes into consciousness is thought by us either as belonging to the mental self exclusively (*subjectivo-subjective*), or as belonging to the not-self exclusively (*objectivo-objective*), or as belonging partly to both (*subjectivo-objective*).

(B) THE RELATIONS OF EXISTENCE are either *intrinsic* or *extrinsic*.

I. The *intrinsic*, which may also be called the *qualitative*, relation is that of *Substance* and *Quality* (quality being variously styled *form*, *accident*, *prop-*

erty, mode, affection, phenomenon, appearance, attribute, predicate, denomination, etc.). Substance and Quality are manifestly only thought as mutual *relatives.*

1. We cannot think a *quality existing absolutely,* in or of itself; we are constrained to think it as inhering in some basis, substratum, hypostasis, subject, or substance.

2. But this *substance* cannot be conceived by us, except negatively, that is, as the unapparent, — the inconceivable correlative of certain appearing qualities. If we attempt to think it positively, we can think it only by transforming it into a quality or bundle of qualities, which, again, we are compelled to refer to an unknown substance, now necessarily supposed for their incogitable basis.

Everything in fact may be conceived as the quality or as the substance of something else. But absolute substance and absolute quality, — these are both inconceivable, as more than negations of the conceivable.

II. The *extrinsic* relation of existence may be called *quantitative,* and is threefold, as constituted by three species of quantity, — *Time, Space,* and *Degree.*

i. *Time, Protension,* or *Protensive quantity,* called likewise *Duration,* is a necessary condition of thought. It may be considered both (1.) in itself, and (2.) in the things which it contains.

1. *In itself,* —

(a) Time is *positively inconceivable, firstly,* either, (α) on the one hand, as *absolute,* that is, absolutely commencing or absolutely terminating, or (β) on the

other hand, as *infinite* or eternal, whether *ab ante* or
a post; it is no less inconceivable, *secondly*, if we attempt (*α*) to fix an *absolute* minimum or (*β*) to follow out an *infinite* division.

(*b*) Time is *positively conceivable*, if conceived,
firstly, as an indefinite past, present, or future, or, *secondly*, as an indeterminate mean between the two
unthinkable extremes of an absolute least and an infinite divisibility ; for thus it is *relative*.

2. *Things in Time* are either, *firstly*, *coinclusive*,
when, (*a*) if of the same time they are, *pro tanto*, identical apparently and in thought, (*b*) if of different times
(as causes and effect, *causæ et causatum*), they appear
as different but are thought identical ; or, *secondly*,
they are *coexclusive*, when they are mutually either
prior and *posterior* or *contemporaneous*. The impossibility of thinking as non-existent in time (either past
or future) aught which we have conceived as existent,
affords the principle of *Causality*, etc.[1]

ii. *Space, Extension,* or *Extensive quantity* is, in like
manner, a necessary condition of thought, and may
also be considered both (1.) in itself and (2.) in the
things which it contains.

1. *In itself,* —

(*a*) Space is *positively inconceivable*, *firstly*, as a
whole, either (*α*) *infinitely* unbounded or (*β*) *absolutely*
bounded ; *secondly*, as a part, either (*α*) *infinitely*
divisible or (*β*) *absolutely* indivisible.

(*b*) Space is *positively conceivable* as a mean be-

---

[1] See this principle developed in the Appendix to this Chapter. —
J. C. M.

tween these extremes, that is, either as an indefinite whole or as an indefinite part; for thus it is *relative*.

2. The *things in Space* may be considered, *firstly*, in relation to Space itself, when the extension occupied by a thing is called its *place*, and a thing changing its place gives the relation of *motion*. Considered, *secondly*, in relation to each other, they are either (*a*) *inclusive*, thus originating the relation of *containing* and *contained*, or (*b*) *coexclusive*, thus determining the relation of position or situation, — of here and there (*Ubication*). On Space are dependent what are called the *Primary* Qualities of body, strictly so denominated, and Space combined with Degree affords, of body, the *Secundo-primary* Qualities. Our inability to conceive an absolute elimination from space of aught which we have conceived to occupy space, gives the law of what I have called *Ultimate Incompressibility*, etc.[1]

iii. *Degree, Intension*, or *Intensive quantity* is not, like Time and Space, an absolute condition of thought. It may therefore be thought as null, or as existing only potentially. But thinking it to be, we must think it as a quantity; and, as a quantity, it is positively both inconceivable and conceivable.

1. *In itself*, —

(*a*) Degree is *positively inconceivable*, (*a*) *absolutely*, either as least or as greatest, (*β*) *infinitely*, either in increase or diminution; but

(*b*) It is *positively conceivable*, in so far as it is

---

[1] See above, Chap. I., § 1. (B). — J. C. M.

conceived as *relative*, — as indefinitely high or higher, as indefinitely low or lower.

2. The *things thought under Degree*, (*a*) if of the same intension, are correlatively uniform; (*b*) if of a different degree, are correlatively higher or lower.

Degree is developed into the *Secondary* Qualities of body, and, combined with Space, into the *Secundo-primary*.[1] (*Discussions*, pp. 602–8. Compare *Lect. on Metaph.*, XXXVIII.) (On the next page is given a tabular view of the above conditions of thought.)

APPENDIX TO CHAPTER VI.

LAW OF THE CONDITIONED IN ITS APPLICATION TO THE PRINCIPLE OF CAUSALITY.

To manifest the utility of introducing the principle of the Conditioned into our metaphysical speculations, I shall (always in outline) give one only, but that a signal illustration of its importance.

Of all questions in the history of philosophy, that concerning the origin of our judgment of *Cause and Effect* is perhaps the most celebrated; but, strange to say, there is not, so far as I am aware, to be found a comprehensive view of the various theories proposed in explanation, — not to say, among these, any satisfactory explanation of the phenomenon itself.

The phenomenon is this: When aware of a new appearance, we are *unable* to conceive that therein

---

[1] See the preceding note. — J. C. M.

CONDITIONS OF THE THINKABLE SYSTEMATIZED.

POSITIVE THOUGHT, i. e., thought in which existence is mentally affirmed, is realized under

- (§1.) THE CONDITION OF NON-CONTRADICTION, giving *The Not-impossible in reality and in thought,* under its three rules of
  - (1.) *Identity.*
  - (2.) *Contradiction.*
  - (3.) *Excluded Middle.*

- (§2.) THE CONDITION OF RELATIVITY, *giving The Possible to Thought,* under Relations,
  - *Necessary and Primary,*
    - (A) *Of Knowledge,* i. e., between SUBJECT AND OBJECT, as the condition of *knowing.*
  - *Contingent and Derivative,* which may be variously classified, but of which no classification can be here detailed.
    - (B) *Of Existence,* i. e., in Objects, as conditions of *being known,* comprising those that are
      - I. *Intrinsic or Qualitative,* i. e., of SUBSTANCE AND QUALITY.
        - i. *Protensive,* i. e., TIME, applying to both Substance and Quality.
      - II. *Extrinsic or Quantitative,* and those of Quantity
        - ii. *Extensive,* i. e., SPACE, applying to Substance.
        - iii. *Intensive,* i. e., DEGREE, applying to Quality.

has originated any new existence, and are therefore *constrained* to think that what now appears to us under a new form, had previously an existence under others — others conceivable by us or not. These others (for they are always plural) are called its *cause;* and a cause, or more properly causes, we cannot but suppose ; for a cause is simply everything without which the effect would not result, and all such concurring, the effect cannot but result. We are utterly unable to realize in thought the possibility of the complement of existence being either increased or diminished. We are unable, on the one hand, to conceive nothing becoming something, or, on the other, something becoming nothing. When God is said to create out of nothing, we construe this to thought by supposing that he evolves existence out of nothing but himself; and in like manner we conceive annihilation only by conceiving the Creator to withdraw his creation, by withdrawing his creative energy from actuality into power.

> —— "Nil posse creari
> De Nihilo, neque quod genitu 'st ad Nil revocari;"
> —— "Gigni
> De Nihilo Nihil, in Nihilum Nil posse reverti."

These lines of Lucretius and Persius enounce a physical axiom of antiquity, which, when interpreted by the doctrine of the Conditioned, is itself at once recalled into harmony with revealed truth, and, expressing in its purest form the conditions of human thought, expresses also implicitly the whole intellectual phenomenon of causality.

There is thus conceived an absolute tautology between the effect and its causes. We think the causes to contain all that is contained in the effect; the effect to contain nothing which was not contained in the causes. Take an example. A neutral salt is an effect of the conjunction of an acid and an alkali. Here we do not, and here we cannot, conceive that, in effect, any new existence has been added, nor can we conceive that any has been taken away. But another example: Gunpowder is the effect of a mixture of sulphur, charcoal, and nitre; and these three substances are again the effect of simpler constituents, and these constituents again of simpler elements, either known or conceived to exist. Now, in all this series of compositions, we cannot conceive that aught begins to exist. The gunpowder, the last compound, we are compelled to think, contains precisely the same quantum of existence that its ultimate elements contained prior to their combination. Well; we explode the powder. Can we conceive that existence has been diminished by the annihilation of a single element previously in being, or increased by the addition of a single element which was not heretofore in nature? "Omnia mutantur; nihil interit," is what we think, what we must think. This, then, is the mental phenomenon of causality, — that we necessarily deny in thought that the object, which appears to begin to be, really so begins; and that we necessarily identify its present with its past existence. Here it is not requisite that we should know under what form, under what combinations, this existence was previously realized; in other words, it is not requisite that we should know what are the particular causes of the particular effect. The discovery of the connection of determinate causes and determinate effects is merely contingent and individual, — merely the datum of experience; but the principle that every event should have its causes is necessary and universal, and is imposed on us as a condition of our human intelligence itself. This necessity of so thinking is the only phenomenon to be explained.

The opinions in regard to the nature and origin of the principle of causality fall into two great categories. The first category (A) comprehends those theories which consider this principle as Empirical, or *à posteriori*, that is, as *derived from experience;* the other (B) comprehends those which view it as Pure, or *à priori*, that is, as *a condition of intelligence itself.* These two primary genera are, however, severally subdivided into various subordinate classes.

The former category (A), under which this principle is regarded as *the result of experience*, contains *two classes*, inasmuch as the causal judgment may be supposed founded either (I.) on an *Original*, or (II.) on a *Derivative*, cognition. Each of these again is divided into two, according as the principle is supposed to have an *objective*, or a *subjective*, origin. In the former case, that is, where the cognition is supposed to be original and underived, it is Objective, or rather Objectivo-Objective; when held to consist in an *immediate perception of the power or efficacy of causes in the external and internal worlds* (1.); and Subjective, or rather Objectivo-Subjective, when viewed as given in *a self-consciousness alone of the power or efficacy of our own volitions* (2.). In the

12

latter case, that is, where the cognition is supposed to be derivative; if *objective*, it is viewed as *a product of Induction and Generalization* (3.); if *subjective, of Association and Custom* (4.).

In like manner, the latter category (B), under which the causal principle is considered *not as a result, but as a condition, of experience*, is variously divided and subdivided. In the first place, the opinions under this category fall into *two classes*, inasmuch as some regard the causal judgment (I.) as an *Ultimate* or *Primary* law of mind, while others regard it (II.) as a *Secondary* or *Derived*. Those who hold the former doctrine, in viewing it as a simple original principle, hold likewise that it is a positive act, — an affirmative datum of intelligence. This class is finally subdivided into *two opinions*. For some hold that the causal judgment, as necessary, is given in what they call "*the principle of Causality*," that is, *the principle which declares that everything which begins to be must have its cause* (5.); while at least one philosopher, without explicitly denying that the causal judgment is necessary, would identify it with the principle of our "*Expectation of the Constancy of Nature*" (6.).

Those who hold that it can be analyzed into a higher principle, also hold that it is not of a positive, but of a negative, character. These, however, are divided into two classes. By some it has been maintained, that *the principle of Causality can be resolved into the principle of Contradiction* (7.), which, as I formerly stated, ought in propriety to be called the principle of Non-Contradiction. On the other hand, it may be (though it never has been) argued, that *the judgment of Causality can be analyzed into what I called the principle of the Conditioned, — the principle of relativity* (8.). To one or the other of these eight heads all the doctrines that have been actually maintained in regard to the origin of the principle in question, may be referred; and the classification is the better worthy of your attention, as in no work will you find any attempt at even an enumeration of the various theories, actual and possible, on this subject. (The table on the next page affords a general conspectus of these theories.)

An adequate discussion of these several heads, and a special consideration of the differences of the individual opinions which they comprehend, would far exceed our limits. I shall, therefore, confine myself to a few observations on the value of these eight doctrines in general, without descending to the particular modifications under which they have been maintained by particular philosophers.

(A) THEORIES WHICH DERIVE THE CAUSAL JUDGMENT FROM EXPERIENCE. Of these,

I. The first two, — (1.) that which asserts *that we have a perception of causal agency as we have a perception of external objects;* and (2.) that which maintains *that we are self-conscious of efficiency,* — have been always held in combination, though the second has been frequently held by philosophers who have abandoned the first as untenable. Considering them together, that is, as forming the opinion that we directly and immediately apprehend the efficiency of causes, both external and internal, — this opinion is refuted by two objections. The first is, that we have no such

SCHEME OF THEORIES AS TO THE ORIGIN OF THE CAUSAL JUDGMENT.

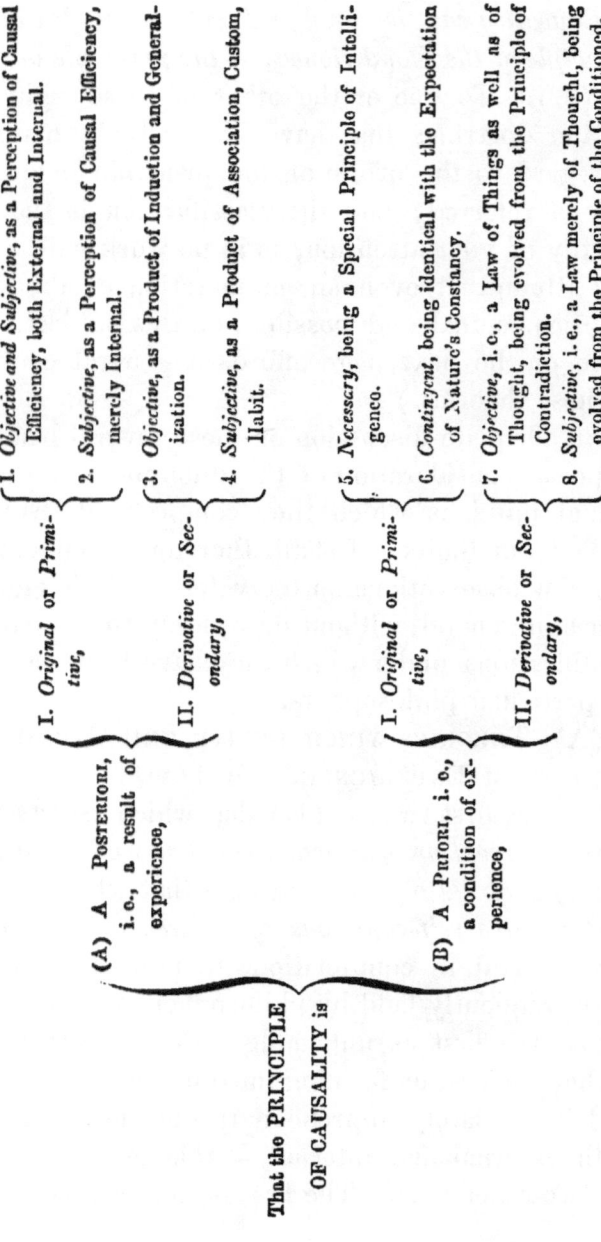

That the PRINCIPLE OF CAUSALITY is

(A) A Posteriori, i.e., a result of experience,

I. *Original* or *Primitive*,

1. *Objective and Subjective*, as a Perception of Causal Efficiency, both External and Internal.

2. *Subjective*, as a Perception of Causal Efficiency, merely Internal.

II. *Derivative* or *Secondary*,

3. *Objective*, as a Product of Induction and Generalization.

4. *Subjective*, as a Product of Association, Custom, Habit.

(B) A Priori, i.e., a condition of experience,

I. *Original* or *Primitive*,

5. *Necessary*, being a Special Principle of Intelligence.

6. *Contingent*, being identical with the Expectation of Nature's Constancy.

II. *Derivative* or *Secondary*,

7. *Objective*, i.e., a Law of Things as well as of Thought, being evolved from the Principle of Contradiction.

8. *Subjective*, i.e., a Law merely of Thought, being evolved from the Principle of the Conditioned.

apprehension; the second, that if we had, this being merely empirical, merely conversant with individual instances, could never account for the quality of necessity and universality which accompanies the judgment of causality.

(a) *First objection,* (1.) *as against the first theory.* In regard to the first of these objections, it is now universally admitted, that we have no perception of the connection of cause and effect in the external world. For example; when one billiard-ball is seen to strike another, we perceive only that the impulse of the one is followed by the motion of the other, but have no perception of any force or efficiency in the first, by which it is connected with the second, in the relation of causality. Hume was the philosopher who decided the opinion of the world on this point. He was not, however, the first who stated the fact, or even the reasoner who stated it most clearly. I could adduce a whole army of philosophers previous to Hume who had announced and illustrated the fact.

First objection, (2.) *as against the second theory.* There are many philosophers who surrender the external perception, and maintain our internal consciousness, of causation or power. This opinion was, in one chapter of his *Essay,* advanced by Locke, and, at a very recent date, it has been amplified and enforced with distinguished ability by the late M. Maine de Biran, one of the acutest metaphysicians of France. On this doctrine, the notion of cause is not given to us by the observations of external phenomena, which, as considered only by the senses, manifest no causal efficiency, and appear to us only as successive; it is

given to us within, in reflection, in the consciousness
of our operations and of the power which exerts them,
— namely, the will. I make an effort to move my
arm, and I move it. When we analyze attentively
the phenomenon of *effort*, which M. de Biran considers
as the type of the phenomena of volition, the following are the results: 1°, The consciousness of an
act of will; 2°, The consciousness of a motion produced; 3°, A relation of the motion to the volition.
And what is this relation? Not a simple relation of
succession. The will is not for us a pure act without
efficiency, — it is a productive energy; so that, in a
volition, there is given to us the notion of cause; and
this notion we subsequently project out from our internal activities, into the changes of the external
world.

This reasoning, in so far as regards the mere empirical fact of our consciousness of causality, in the relation of our will as moving, and of our limbs as moved,
is refuted by the consideration, that between the overt
fact of corporeal movement of which we are cognizant,
and the internal act of mental determination of which
we are also cognizant, there intervenes a numerous
series of intermediate agencies of which we have no
knowledge; and, consequently, that we can have no
consciousness of any causal connection between the
extreme links of this chain, — the volition to move
and the limb moving, as this hypothesis asserts. No
one is immediately conscious, for example, of moving
his arm through his volition. Previously to this ultimate movement, muscles, nerves, a multitude of solid
and fluid parts, must be set in motion by the will;

but of this motion we know, from consciousness, absolutely nothing. A person struck with paralysis is conscious of no inability in his limb to fulfil the determinations of his will; and it is only after having willed, and finding that his limbs do not obey his volition, that he learns by his experience, that the external movement does not follow the internal act. But as the paralytic learns after the volition that his limbs do not obey his mind; so it is only after volition that the man in health learns that his limbs do obey the mandates of his will.

(*b*) The *Second Objection,* mentioned above, is fatal to the theory which would found the judgment of causality on any empirical cognition, whether of the phenomena of mind or of the phenomena of matter. Admitting that causation were cognizable, and that perception and self-consciousness were competent to its apprehension, still, as these faculties could only take note of individual causations, we should be wholly unable, out of such empirical acts, to evolve the quality of necessity and universality, by which this notion is distinguished. Admitting that we had really observed the agency of any number of causes, still this would not explain to us how we are unable to think a manifestation of existence without thinking it as an effect. Our internal experience, especially in the relation of our volitions to their effects, may be useful in giving us a clearer notion of causality: but it is altogether incompetent to account for what in it there is of the quality of necessity.

II. As the first and second opinions have been usually associated, so also have the third and fourth;

that is, the doctrine *that our notion of causality is the
offspring of the objective principle of Induction or Generalization*, and the doctrine *that it is the offspring of
the subjective principle of Association or Custom.*

3. In regard to the former, it is plain that the observation that certain phenomena are found to succeed
certain other phenomena, and the generalization consequent thereon, that these are reciprocally causes and
effects, could never of itself have engendered, not
only the strong, but the irresistible belief, that every
event must have its cause. Each of these observations is contingent : and any number of observed contingencies will never impose upon us the feeling of
necessity, — of our inability to think the opposite.
Nay, more, this theory evolves the absolute notion
of causality out of the observation of a certain number
of uniform consecutions among phenomena; that is,
it would collect that *all must be*, because *some are*.
But we find no difficulty whatever in conceiving the
reverse of all or any of the consecutions we have observed; and yet the general notion of causality,
which, *ex hypothesi*, is their result, we cannot possibly
think as possibly unreal. We have always seen a
stone fall to the ground when thrown into the air;
but we find no difficulty in representing to ourselves
the possibility of one or all stones gravitating from
the earth; only we cannot conceive the possibility
of this, or any other event, happening without a
cause.

4. Nor does the latter afford a better solution.
The *necessity* of so thinking cannot be derived from a
custom of so thinking. Allow the force of custom to

be great as may be, still it is always limited to the customary; and the *customary* has nothing whatever in it of the *necessary*. But we have here to account not for a strong, but *for an absolutely irresistible belief.* On this theory, also, the causal judgment, when association is recent, should be weak, and should only gradually acquire its full force in proportion as custom becomes inveterate. But do we find that the causal judgment is weaker in the young, stronger in the old? There is no difference. In either case, there is no less and no more; the necessity in both is absolute.

(B) THEORIES WHICH MAINTAIN THE CAUSAL JUDGMENT TO BE A DELIVERANCE OF INTELLIGENCE. Of the four opinions comprised under this category,

I. The first two agree in holding that the causal judgment may be identified with a *primary* intellectual principle.

5. Of these, the first (the fifth in general) maintains that this principle is *necessary*, making its rejection in thought impossible. To this are to be referred the relative theories of Descartes, Leibnitz, Kames, Reid, Kant, Fichte, Bouterweck, Jacobi, Stewart, Cousin, and the majority of modern philosophers. Now, without descending into details, it is manifest in general, that against the assumption of a special principle, which this doctrine makes, there exists a primary presumption of philosophy. This is the Law of Parcimony, which forbids, without necessity, the multiplication of entities, powers, principles, or causes; above all, the postulation of an unknown force where a known impotence can account for the

phenomenon. We are, therefore, entitled to apply Occam's razor to this theory of causality, unless it be proved impossible to explain the causal judgment at a cheaper rate, by deriving it from a higher, and that a negative, origin. On a doctrine like the present is thrown the onus of vindicating its necessity, by showing that, unless a special and positive principle be assumed, there exists no competent mode to save the phenomena. It can only, therefore, be admitted provisorily; and it falls of course, if the phenomenon it would explain can be explained on less onerous conditions. Leaving, therefore, this theory, which certainly does account for the phenomenon, to fall or stand, according as either of the two last opinions be, or be not, found sufficient, I go on to that preceding these.

6. Dr. Brown has promulgated a doctrine of Causality, which may be numbered as the sixth; though perhaps it is hardly deserving of distinct enumeration. He actually identifies the causal judgment, which to us is *necessary*, with the principle by which we are *merely inclined* to believe in the uniformity of nature's operations. But apart from all subordinate objections, it is sufficient to say that the phenomenon to be explained is the *necessity* of thinking, — the absolute *impossibility* of not thinking, — a cause; whilst all that the latter pretends to is, *to incline us to expect that like antecedents will be followed by like consequents.* This necessity to suppose a cause for every phenomenon, Dr. Brown, if he does not expressly deny, keeps cautiously out of view, virtually, in fact,

eliminating all that requires explanation in the problem.

II. The two remaining theories agree with the fifth and sixth in regarding the causal judgment as of *à priori* origin, but differ from them in viewing it as *derivative* and *secondary*. Of these two theories,

7. The first attempts to establish the principle of Causality upon the principle of Contradiction. Listen to the pretended demonstration : Whatever is produced without a cause, is produced by nothing, in other words, has nothing for its cause. But nothing can no more be a cause than it can be something. The same intuition, which makes us aware that nothing is not something, shows us that everything must have a real cause of its existence. To this it is sufficient to say, that the existence of causes being the point in question, the existence of causes must not be taken for granted in the very reasoning which attempts to prove their reality. In excluding causes, we exclude *all* causes ; and consequently exclude "*nothing*" considered as a cause ; it is not, therefore, allowable, contrary to that exclusion, *to suppose* "*nothing*" *as a cause*, and then from the absurdity of that supposition to infer the absurdity of the exclusion itself. If everything must have a cause, it follows that, upon the exclusion of other causes, we must accept of nothing as a cause. But it is the very point at issue, whether everything must have a cause or not ; and, therefore, it violates the first principles of reasoning to take this *quæsitum* itself as granted. This opinion is now universally abandoned.

8. The eighth and last opinion is that which re-

gards the judgment of causality as derived; and
derives it not from a power, but from an impotence,
of mind; in a word, from the principle of the Conditioned.   I do not think it possible, without a detailed exposition of the various categories of thought,
to make you fully understand the grounds and bear-
ings of this opinion.   In attempting to explain, you
must, therefore, allow me to take for granted certain
laws of thought, to which I have only been able inci-
dentally to allude.   Those, however, which I postulate, are such as are now generally admitted by all
philosophers who allow the mind itself to be a source
of cognitions; and the only one which has not been
recognized by them, but which, as I endeavored
briefly to prove, must likewise be taken into account,
is the Law of the Conditioned, *that the conceivable has
always two opposite extremes, and that the extremes are
equally inconceivable.*

Philosophers, who allow a native principle to the
mind at all, allow that Existence is such a principle.
I shall, therefore, take for granted Existence as the
highest category or condition of thought.   All that
we perceive or imagine as different from us, we perceive or imagine as objectively existent.   All that
we are conscious of as an act or modification of self,
we are conscious of only as subjectively existent.   All
thought, therefore, implies the thought of existence.
As a second category or subjective condition of
thought, I postulate that of Time.   This likewise
cannot be denied me.   It is the necessary condition
of every conscious act; thought is only realized to us
as in succession, and succession is only conceived by

us under the concept of time. Existence and Existence in Time is thus an elementary form of our intelligence. But we do not conceive existence in time absolutely or infinitely, — we conceive it only as *conditioned in time;* and *Existence Conditioned in Time* expresses, at once and in relation, the three categories of thought which afford us in combination the principle of Causality. This requires some explanation.

When we perceive or imagine an object, we perceive or imagine it (1.) As existent, and (2.) As in Time; Existence and Time being categories of all thought. But what is meant by saying, I perceive, or imagine, or, in general, think an object only as I perceive, or imagine, or, in general, think it to exist? Simply this: that, as thinking it, I cannot but think it to exist, in other words, that *I cannot annihilate it in thought.* I may think away from it, I may turn to other things, and I can thus exclude it from my consciousness; but, actually thinking it, I cannot think it as non-existent, for as it is thought, so it is thought existent.

But a thing is thought to exist, only as it is thought to exist in time. Time is present, past, and future. We cannot think an object of thought as non-existent *de presenti.* But can we think that quantum of existence of which an object, real or ideal, is the complement, as non-existent, either in time past, or in time future? Make the experiment. Try to think the object of your thought as non-existent in the moment before the present. You cannot. Try it in the moment before that. You cannot. Nor can you annihilate it by carrying it back to any moment, however

distant in the past. You may conceive the parts of
which this complement of existence is composed, as
separated; if a material object, you can think it as
shivered to atoms, sublimated into ether; but not
one iota of existence can you conceive as annihilated,
which subsequently you thought to exist. In like
manner, try the future, — try to conceive the prospec-
tive annihilation of any present object, of any atom
of any present object. You cannot. All this may be
possible, but of it we cannot think the possibility.
But if you can thus conceive neither the absolute commencement nor the absolute termination of anything
that is once thought to exist, try, on the other hand,
if you can conceive the opposite alternative of infinite
non-commencement, or of infinite non-termination.
To this you are equally impotent. This is the category of the Conditioned as applied to the category of
Existence under the category of Time.

But in this application is the principle of Causality
not given? Why, what is the law of Causality? Simply this, — that, when an object is presented phenom-
enally as commencing, we cannot but suppose that
the complement of existence, which it now contains, has previously been; in other words, that all
that we at present come to know as an effect must
previously have existed in its causes; though what
these causes are, we may perhaps be altogether unable even to surmise. (*Lect. on Metaph.*, XXXIX.,
and *Discussions*, pp. 609–622. Compare also *Lect.
on Metaph.*, XL.)

SECOND PART OF PHENOMENAL PSYCHOLOGY.

PHENOMENOLOGY OF THE FEELINGS.

SECOND PART OF PHENOMENAL PSYCHOLOGY.

PHENOMENOLOGY OF THE FEELINGS.

INTRODUCTION.

In entering on the second great class of mental phenomena, there is a preliminary question to be disposed of: What is the position of the Feelings by reference to the two other classes; and, in particular, should the consideration of the Feelings precede or follow that of the Conations?

To resolve this problem let us take an example. A person is fond of cards. In a company, where he beholds a game in progress, there arises a desire to join in it. Now, the desire is here manifestly kindled by the pleasure which the person had and has in the play. The feeling thus connects the cognition of the play with the desire to join in it; it forms the bridge, and contains the motive, by which we are roused from mere knowledge to appetency, — to conation, by reference to which we move ourselves so as to attain the end in view.

Thus we find, in actual life, the Feelings intermediate between the Cognitions and the Conations. And

this relative position of the several powers is necessary : without the previous cognition, there could be
neither feeling nor conation ; and without the previous feeling there could be no conation. For if the
mere cognition of a thing were sufficient to rouse conation, then it is evident (1.) that all objects, known
in the same manner and in the same degree, would
become equally the objects of desire and will ; while
(2.) all persons would desire an object equally, as
long as their cognition of the object remained the
same.

Our conclusion, therefore, is, that as in our actual
existence the feelings find their place after the cognitions and before the conations, so in the science of
mind the theory of the feelings ought to follow that
of our faculties of knowledge, and to precede that of
our faculties of will and desire.

CHAPTER I.

ABSTRACT THEORY OF PLEASURE AND PAIN.

I PROCEED to deliver the theory of pleasure and pain.

I. Man exists only as he lives; as an intelligent and sensible being, he consciously lives, but this only as he consciously energizes. Human existence is only a more general expression for human life, and human life only a more general expression for the sum of energies in which that life is realized, and through which it is manifested in consciousness.

Observation. The term *energy* is here used to comprehend all the mixed states of action and passion of which we are conscious.

II. Human existence, human life, human energy, is not unlimited, but on the contrary determined to a certain number of modes, through which alone it can possibly be exerted. These different modes of action are called, in different relations, *powers, faculties, capacities, dispositions, habits.*

III. Man, as he consciously exists, is the subject of pleasure and pain; and these of various kinds;

but as man consciously exists in and through the
exertion of certain determinate powers, so it is only
through the exertion of these powers that he becomes
the subject of pleasure and pain ; each power being
in itself at once the faculty of a specific energy, and
a capacity of an appropriate pleasure or pain, as the
concomitant of that energy.

IV. The energy of each power of conscious existence having, as its reflex or concomitant, an appropriate pleasure or pain, and no pleasure or pain being
competent to man, except as the concomitant of some
determinate energy of life, the all-important question
arises : What is the general law under which these
counter-phenomena appear in all their special manifestations?

V. The answer to this question is : the more
perfect, the more pleasurable, the energy ; the more
imperfect, the more painful.

VI. The perfection of an energy is twofold : (1.)
subjective, by relation to the power of which it is the
exertion ; (2.) *objective*, by relation to the object
about which it is conversant.

VII. (1.) *By relation to its power*, an energy is
perfect, when it is tantamount (*a*) to the full, and (*b*)
not to more than the full, complement of free and
spontaneous energy which the power is capable of
exerting ; an energy is imperfect, either (*a*) when
the power is restrained from putting forth the whole
amount of energy it would otherwise tend to do, or
(*b*) when it is stimulated to put forth a larger amount
than that to which it is spontaneously disposed.

The amount of energy in the case of a *single power*

is of two kinds, (*a*) *intensive*, (*b*) *protensive*. A perfect energy is, therefore, that which is evolved by a power, both in the degree and for the continuance to which it is competent without straining; an imperfect energy, that which is evolved by a power in a lower or in a higher degree, for a shorter or for a longer continuance than, if left to itself, it would freely exert.

When we look to complex states in which a *plurality of powers* may be simultaneously called into action, we have, besides (*a*) the *intensive* and (*b*) *protensive* quantities of energy, (*c*) a third kind, to wit, the *extensive* quantity. A state is said to contain a greater amount of extensive energy, in proportion as it forms the complement of a greater number of simultaneously co-operating powers. This complement, it is evident, may be conceived as made up either of energies all intensively and protensively perfect and pleasurable; or of energies all intensively and protensively imperfect and painful; or of energies partly perfect, partly imperfect; and this in every combination afforded by the various perfections and imperfections of the intensive and protensive quantities.

It may be here noticed that the intensive and the two other quantities stand always in an inverse ratio to each other; that is, the higher the degree of any energy, the shorter is its continuance, and, during its continuance, the more completely does it constitute the whole mental state.

VIII. (2.) *By relation to the object* about which it is conversant (and by *object* is here denoted every objective cause by which a power is determined to

activity), an energy is perfect, when this object is of
such a character as to afford to its power the condition
requisite to let it spring to full spontaneous activity;
imperfect, when the object is of such a character as
either (*a*) to stimulate the power to a degree or to a
continuance of activity beyond its maximum of free
exertion; or (*b*) to thwart it in its tendency towards
this its natural limit. An object is consequently
pleasurable or painful, inasmuch as it determines a
power to perfect or to imperfect energy.

But an object, or plurality of objects simultaneously
presented, may determine a plurality of powers into
co-activity. The complex state, which thus arises, is
pleasurable in proportion as its constitutive energies
are severally more perfect; painful in proportion as
these are more imperfect: and in proportion as an
object, or a complement of objects, occasions the average perfection or the average imperfection of the
complex state, is it, in like manner, pleasurable or
painful.

IX. In conformity to this doctrine, pleasure and
pain may be thus defined: PLEASURE *is a reflex of the
spontaneous and unimpeded exertion of a power, of
whose energy we are conscious;* PAIN, *a reflex of the
overstrained or repressed exertion of such a power.*

Observations. I. In illustration of these definitions
it may be observed that,

1. Pleasure is defined to be the *reflex* of perfect
energy, and not to be either energy or the perfection
of energy itself; and why? (*a*) It is not simply defined an energy, because some energies are not pleasurable, being either painful or indifferent. (*b*) It is

not simply defined the perfection of an energy, because we can easily separate in thought the perfection of an act from any feeling of pleasure in its performance. The same holds true, *mutatis mutandis*, of the definition of pain, as a reflex of imperfect energy.

2. The term *spontaneous* refers to the *subjective*, the term *unimpeded* to the *objective*, perfection.

3. There are powers in man, the activities of which lie beyond the sphere of consciousness;[1] but it is of the very essence of pleasure and pain to be felt, and there is no feeling out of consciousness.

II. It is also to be observed that, on this doctrine, there are different kinds of pleasure and pain.

1. In the first place, these are twofold, inasmuch as each is either *positive* and *absolute* or *negative* and *relative*. (*a*) The mere negation of pain does, by relation to pain, constitute a state of pleasure. Thus the removal of toothache replaces us in a state which, though one really of indifference, is, by contrast to our previous agony, felt as pleasurable. This is negative or relative pleasure. (*b*) Positive or absolute pleasure, on the contrary, is all that pleasure which we feel above a state of indifference, and which is therefore prized as a good in itself, and not simply as the removal of an evil. On the same principle pain is also divided.

2. But, in the second place, there is a subdivision of positive pain into (*a*) that which accompanies a repression of the spontaneous energy of a power, and (*b*) that which is conjoined with its effort when stimulated to over-activity. (*Lect. on Metaph.*, XLII.)

---

[1] See *Phenomenology of the Cognitions*, Chap. II., § 1.

CHAPTER II.

THE ABSTRACT THEORY APPLIED TO THE CONCRETE PHENOMENA: CLASSIFICATION OF THE FEELINGS.

WE may consider the feelings either as *causes* or as *effects*. (1.) As *causes*, they are viewed in relation to their product, — pleasure, or pain. (2.) As *effects*, they are viewed as themselves products of the action of our different constitutive functions.

§ 1. *THE FEELINGS AS CAUSES.*

In this point of view, the feelings are distributed simply into the *pleasurable* and the *painful;* and it remains, on the theory I have proposed, to explain in general the causes of these opposite affections, without descending to their special kinds.

I. The theory meets with no contradiction from the facts of actual life; for the contradictions, which at first sight these seem to offer, prove, when examined, to be real confirmations. Thus it might be thought that the aversion from exercise, — the love of idleness, — in a word, the *dolce far niente*, — is a proof

200

that the inactivity, rather than the exertion, of our powers is the condition of our pleasurable feelings. This objection, from a natural proneness to inertion in man, is superficial. Is the *far niente* — is that doing nothing, in which so many find so sincere a gratification — in reality a negation of activity, and not in truth itself an activity intense and varied? To do nothing, in this sense, is simply to do nothing irksome, especially to do no outward work. But is the mind internally, the while, unoccupied and inert? This, on the contrary, may be vividly alive, — may be intently engaged in the spontaneous play of imagination ; and so far, therefore, in this case, from pleasure being the concomitant of inactivity, the activity is at once vigorous and unimpeded, and such accordingly. as, on our theory, would be accompanied by a high degree of pleasure. *Ennui* is the state on which we find nothing to exercise our powers ; but ennui is a state of pain.

II. A strong confirmation of the theory is derived from the phenomena presented by those affections which we emphatically denominate the *painful*.

1. Take, for example, the affection of *grief*, — the sorrow we feel in the loss of a beloved object. Is this affection unaccompanied with pleasure? So far is this from being the case, that the pleasure so greatly predominates over the pain as to produce a mixed emotion, which is far more pleasurable than any other of which the wounded heart is susceptible.

2. In like manner, *fear* is not simply painful. It is a natural disposition, has a tendency to act ; and there is consequently, along with its essential pain, a

certain pleasure as the reflex of its energy. This is finely expressed by Akenside : —

> "Hence, finally, by night
> The village matron round the blazing hearth
> Suspends the infant audience with her tales,
> Breathing astonishment! of witching rhymes
> And evil spirits of the death-bed call
> Of him who robbed the widow and devoured
> The orphan's portion; of unquiet souls
> Risen from the grave to ease the heavy guilt
> Of deeds in life concealed; of shapes that walk
> At dead of night and clank their chains, and wave
> The torch of hell around the murderer's bed.
> At every solemn pause the crowd recoil,
> Gazing each other speechless, and congealed
> With shivering sighs, till, eager for the event,
> Around the beldame all erect they hang,
> Each trembling heart with grateful terrors quelled."

3. *Pity*, also, which, being a sympathetic passion, implies a participation in sorrow, is yet confessedly agreeable. The poet even accords to the energy of this benevolent affection a preference over the enjoyments of an exclusive selfishness : —

> "The broadest mirth unfeeling folly wears
> Is not so sweet as virtue's very tears."

4. On the same principle is to be explained the enjoyment which men have in spectacles of suffering, — in the combats of animals and men, in executions, in tragedies, etc. ; a disposition which not unfrequently becomes an irresistible habit, not only for individuals, but also for nations. The excitation of energetic emotions, painful in themselves, is also pleasurable.

We may here notice four *general causes* which contribute to raise or to lower the intensity of our energies, and consequently to determine the corresponding degree of pleasure or pain.

I. *Novelty.* The principle on which novelty determines a higher energy is twofold; and of these the one may be called the *subjective*, the other the *objective*.

1. In a *subjective* relation, the new is pleasurable, inasmuch as this supposes that the mind is determined to a mode of action, either from inactivity or from another state of energy. (*a*) In the former case, energy, the condition of pleasure, is caused; (*b*) in the latter, a change of energy is afforded, which is also pleasurable; for powers energize less vigorously in proportion to the continuance of the same exertion, and, consequently, a new activity being determined, this replaces a strained or expiring exercise, that is, it replaces a painful, indifferent, or unpleasurable feeling by one of comparatively vivid enjoyment.

2. In an *objective* relation, a novel object is pleasing, because it affords a gratification to our desire of knowledge. The old is already known, and therefore no longer occupies the cognitive faculties; whereas the new, as new, is still unknown, and rouses to energy the powers by which it is to be brought within the system of our knowledge.

II. *Contrast* operates in two ways; for it has the effect of enhancing both the real or absolute, and the apparent or relative, intensity of a feeling. (1.) As an instance of the former, the unkindness of a person, from whom we expect kindness, rouses to a far higher pitch the emotions consequent on injury. (2.) As an instance of the latter, the pleasure of eating appears proportionally great when it is immediately connected and contrasted with the removal of the pangs of hunger.

III. The relation of *harmony* or *discord*, in which one coexistent activity stands to another. At different times we exist in different complex states of feeling, and these states are made up of a number of constituent thoughts and affections. At one time — say during a sacred solemnity — we are in a very different frame of mind from what we are in at another, — say during the representation of a comedy. Now, then, in such a state of mind, if anything occurs to awaken to activity a power previously occupied, or to occupy a power, previously in energy, in a different manner, this new mode of activity is either of the same general character and tendency with the other constituent elements of the complex state, or it is not. (1.) In the former case, the new energy chimes in with the old; each operates without impediment from the other, and the general harmony of feeling is not violated; (2.) in the latter case, the new energy jars with the old, and each severally counteracts and impedes the other. Thus, in the sacred solemnity, and when our minds are brought to a state of serious contemplation, everything that operates in unison with that state — say a pious discourse or a strain of solemn music — will have a greater effect. But suppose that, instead of the pious discourse, or the strain of solemn music, we are treated to a merry tune or a witty address; these, though at another season they

might afford us considerable pleasure, would, under
the circumstances, cause only pain.

IV. *Association.* It is evident, in the *first* place,
that one object, considered simply and in itself, will
be more pleasing than another, in proportion as it, of
its proper nature, determines the exertion of a greater
amount of free energy. But, in the *second* place, the
amount of free energy, which an object may itself
elicit, is small, when compared with the amount that
may be elicited by its train of associated representations. Thus it is evident, that the object, which in
itself would otherwise be pleasing, may, through the
accident of association, be the occasion of pain; and
on the contrary, that an object, naturally indifferent or even painful, may, by the same contingency,
be productive of pleasure.

This principle accounts for a great many of our
intellectual pleasures and pains; but it is far from
accounting for everything. In fact, it supposes, as its
condition, that there are pains and pleasures not
founded on association. Association is a principle of
pleasure and pain, only as it is a principle of energy
of one character or another; and the attempts that
have been made to resolve all our mental pleasures
and pains into association are guilty of a twofold vice.
For (1.) they convert a partial into an exclusive law;
and (2.) they elevate a subordinate into a supreme
principle. (*Lect. on Metaph.*, XLIV.)

The influence of association, by which Mr. Alison
and Lord Jeffrey, among others, have attempted to
explain the whole phenomena of our intellectual
pleasures, was more properly, I think, appreciated by

Hutcheson. "We shall see hereafter," he says, and
Aristotle said the same thing, "that associations of
ideas make objects pleasant and delightful, which are
not naturally apt to give any such pleasures; and the
same way, the casual conjunction of ideas may give a
disgust where there is nothing disagreeable in the
form itself. And this is the occasion of many fantas-
tic aversions to figures of some animals and to some
other forms. Thus swine, serpents of all kinds, and
some insects really beautiful enough, are beheld with
aversion by many people, who have got some accidental ideas associated with them. And for distastes
of this kind no other account can be given."

§ 2. *THE FEELINGS AS EFFECTS.*

Since all feeling is the state in which we are conscious of some of the energies or processes of life, as
these energies or processes differ, so will the correlative feelings: in a word, there will be as many different feelings as there are distinct modes of mental
activity. Now, the feelings, which accompany the
exertion of the bodily powers, whether cognitive or
appetent, will constitute a distinct class, to which we
may with great propriety give the name of *Sensations;*
whereas, on the feelings, which accompany the energies of all our higher powers of mind, we may, with
equal propriety, bestow the name of *Sentiments.*

(A) The Sensations may be divided into two
classes: (1.) those included under what has been
called *Sensus Fixus,* comprehending the five determinate senses of *touch, taste, smell, hearing, sight;* (2.)

those included under what has been called *Sensus Vagus*, comprehending such sensations as those of *heat* and *cold*, of *muscular tension* and *lassitude*, of *hunger* and *thirst*, etc.

I. *Sensus Fixus.* In regard to the determinate senses, each of these organs has its specific action, and its appropriate pleasure or pain. This pleasure and pain, which is that alone belonging to the action of the living organ, and which therefore may be styled *organic*, we must distinguish from that higher feeling, which perhaps results from the exercise of imagination and intellect upon the phenomena delivered by the senses. Thus, I would call *organic* the pleasure we feel in the perception of green or blue, and the pain we feel in the perception of a dazzling white; but I would be perhaps disposed to refer to some other power than the external sense the enjoyment we experience in the harmony of colors, and certainly that which we find in the proportions of figure.

When it is required of us to explain, particularly and in detail, why the rose, for example, produces this sensation of smell, assafœtida that other, and so forth, and to say in what peculiar action does the perfect or pleasurable, and the imperfect or painful, activity of an organ consist, we must at once profess our ignorance. All that we can say is, that, on the general analogy of our being, when the impression of an object on a sense is in harmony with its amount of power, and thus allows it the condition of springing to full spontaneous energy, the result is pleasure; whereas, when the impression is out of harmony with the amount of power, and thus either represses it or stimulates it to over-activity, the result is pain.

II. *Sensus Vagus.* The same explanation must be applied to the sensations which belong to this sense, but in regard to these it is not necessary to say anything in detail.

(B) THE SENTIMENTS may be divided into (1.) the *contemplative*, the concomitants of our cognitive powers, and (2.) the *practical*, the concomitants of our powers of conation.

I. The *contemplative* sentiments are again distributed into (1.) those of the *subsidiary faculties*, and (2.) those of the *elaborative faculty*.

1. The feelings, accompanying the *subsidiary faculties*, may be subdivided into (a) those of *self-consciousness*, and (b) those of *imagination*, comprehending under imagination the relative faculty of *reproduction*.

(a) *Sentiments attending Self-consciousness.* By self-consciousness we become aware that we live. Now, we are conscious of our life only as we are conscious of our activity, and we are conscious of activity only as we are conscious of a change of state; for all activity is the going out of one state into another. Now, if there be nothing which presents to our faculties the objects on which they may exert their activity; in other words, if there be no cause whereby our actual state may be made to pass into another, there results a peculiar irksome feeling of a want of excitement, which we denominate *tedium* or *ennui*. An inability to thought is a security against this feeling, and therefore tedium is far less felt by the uncultivated than by the educated. The more varied the objects presented to our thought, the more varied and vivacious our activity, the intenser will be our consciousness of living, and the more rapidly will the time appear to fly. Hence we explain why we call our easy occupations *pastimes*, and why play is so engaging when it is at all deep. Games of hazard determine a continual change, — now we hope, now we fear; while in games of skill, we experience also the pleasure which arises from the activity of the understanding in carrying through our own, and frustrating the plan of our antagonist.

All that relieves tedium, by affording a change and an easy exercise for our thoughts, causes pleasure. The best cure of tedium is some occupation which, by concentrating our attention on external objects, shall divert it from a retortion on ourselves. All occupation is either labor or play; labor when there is some end ulterior to the activity, play when the activity is for its own sake alone. In both, however, there must be ever and anon a change of object, or both will soon grow tiresome. Labor is thus the best preventive of tedium, for it has an external motive which holds us steadfast to the work; while, after the completion of our task, the feeling of repose, as the change from the feeling of a constrained to that of a spontaneous state, affords a vivid and peculiar pleasure. Labor must alternate with repose, or we shall never know what is the true enjoyment of life.

Thus it appears that a uniform continuity in our internal states is painful, and that pleasure is the result of their commutation. It is, however, to be observed,

14

that the change of our perceptions and thoughts, to be pleasing, must not be too rapid; for as the intervals, when too long, produce the feeling of tedium, so, when too short, they cause that of *giddiness* or *vertigo*. The too rapid passing, for example, of visible objects or of tones before the senses, of images before the phantasy, of thoughts before the understanding, occasions the disagreeable feeling of confusion or stupefaction, which, in individuals of very sensitive temperament, results in *nausea* or *sickness.*

(*b*) *Sentiments attending Imagination.* Whatever in general facilitates the play of imagination, is felt as pleasing; whatever renders it more difficult is felt as displeasing. We are pleased with the portrait of a person whose face we know, if like, because it enables us to recall the features into consciousness easily and freely; and we are displeased with it, if unlike, because it not only does not assist, but thwarts us in our endeavor to recall them; while, after this has been accomplished, we are still further pained by the disharmony we experience between the portrait on the canvas and the representation in our own imagination. A short and characteristic description of things which we have seen pleases us, because, without exacting a protracted effort of attention, and through a few striking traits, it enables the imagination to place the objects vividly before it. On the same principle, whatever facilitates the reproduction of the objects which have been consigned to memory is pleasurable; as, for example, resemblances, contrasts, other associations with the passing thought, metre, rhyme, symmetry, appropriate designations, etc. To realize an act of imagination it is necessary that we comprehend the manifold as a single whole : an object, therefore, which does not allow itself without difficulty to be thus represented in unity, occasions pain ; whereas an object, which can easily be recalled to system, is the cause of pleasure. The former is the case when the object is too large or too complex to be perceived at once, when the parts are not prominent enough to be distinctly impressed on the memory. Order and symmetry, again, facilitate the acts of reproduction and representation, and consequently afford us a proportional gratification. But, on the other hand, as pleasure is in proportion to the amount of free energy, an object which gives no impediment to the comprehensive energy of imagination may not be pleasurable, if it be so simple as not to afford to this faculty a sufficient exercise. Hence it is, that not variety alone, and not unity alone, but variety combined with unity, is that quality in objects, which we emphatically denominate *beautiful*.

2. Under the head of the feelings which are associated with the *elaborative faculty* or the *understanding*, it will be proper to consider, in the first place, those which arise from the operations of the understanding by itself, and afterwards those which accompany the joint exercise of the understanding and the imagination.

(*a*) *Sentiments attending the exercise of the Understanding by itself.* The function of the understanding may in general be said to bestow, on the cognitions which it elaborates, the greatest possible compass, the greatest possible clearness and distinctness, the greatest possible certainty and systematic order; and inasmuch as we approximate to the accomplishment of these ends, we experience pleasure; inasmuch as we meet with hindrances in our attempts, we experience pain. Obscurity and confusion in our cognitions we feel as disagreeable, whereas their clearness and distinctness afford us sincere gratification. We are pained by a hazy and perplexed discourse, but rejoice in one perspicuous and profound. Hence the pleasure we experience in having the cognitions we possessed, but darkling and confused, explicated into life and order; and, on this account, there is hardly a more pleasing object than a tabular conspectus of any complex whole. We are soothed by the solution of a riddle; and the wit which, like a flash of lightning, discovers similarities between objects which seemed contradictory, affords a still intenser enjoyment.

The multitude — the multifarious character — of the objects presented to our observation stands in signal contrast with the very limited capacity of the human intellect. This disproportion constrains us to classify. Now, the process of classification is performed by that function of the understanding which apprehends resemblances. In this detection of the similarities between different objects an energy of the understanding is fully and freely exerted; and hence results a pleasure. But as in general notions the knowledge of individual existences loses in precision and completeness, we again endeavor to find out differences in the things which stand under a notion, to the end that we may be able to specify and individualize them. This counter-process is performed by that function of the understanding which apprehends dissimilarities between resembling objects, and in the full and free exertion of this energy there is a feeling of pleasure.

The intellect further tends to reduce the piecemeal and fragmentary cognitions it possesses to a systematic whole; in other words, to elevate them into *Science*. Hence the pleasure we derive from all that enables us with ease and rapidity to survey the relation of complex parts as constituting the members of one organic whole. The intellect, from the necessity it has of thinking everything as the result of some higher reason, is thus determined to attempt the deduction of every object of cognition from a simple principle. When, therefore, we succeed or seem to succeed in the discovery of such a principle, we feel a pleasure; as we feel a pain when the intellect is frustrated in this endeavor.

To the feelings of pleasure which are afforded by the unimpeded energies of the understanding belongs, likewise, the gratification we find in the apprehension of adaptation of means to ends. Human intelligence is naturally determined to propose to itself an end; and, in the consideration of objects, it thus naturally thinks them under this relation. If, therefore, we consider an object in reference to an end, and if this object be recognized to fulfil the conditions which this relation implies, the act of thought, in which this is accomplished, is an unimpeded and consequently pleasurable energy; whereas the act of cognizing that these conditions are wanting, and the object therefore

ill adapted to its end, is a thwarted, and therefore a
painful, energy of thought.

(*b*) *Sentiments attending the Understanding and
the Imagination in conjunction.* The feelings of satis-
faction which result from the *plastic imagination*, that
is, the phantasy and the understanding conjointly, are
principally those of *beauty* and *sublimity;* and the
judgments which pronounce an object to be *sublime,
beautiful*, etc., are called, by a metaphorical expression, *Judgments of Taste.* They have also been called
Æsthetical Judgments; but both terms are unsatis-
factory. In the following observations it is almost
needless to observe that I can make no attempt at
more than a simple indication of the origin of the
pleasure we derive from the contemplation of those
objects, which, from the character of the feelings they
determine, are called *beautiful, sublime, picturesque*,
etc.

i. *The Beautiful* has been divided into the *free* or
absolute, and the *dependent* or *relative.* In the former
case it is not necessary to have a notion of what the object ought to be before we pronounce it beautiful, or not ;
in the latter case such a previous notion is required.
We judge, for example, a flower to be beautiful,
though unaware of its destination, and that it contains
a complex apparatus of organs all admirably adapted
to the propagation of the plant. When we are made
cognizant of this, we obtain, indeed, an additional
gratification, but one wholly different from that which
we experience in the contemplation of the flower
itself, apart from all consideration of its adaptations.
This distinction appears to me unsound. What has

been distinguished as dependent or relative beauty is nothing more than a beautified utility or a utilized beauty. Be this, however, as it may, our pleasure in both cases arises from a free and full play being allowed to our cognitive faculties.

(*a*) In the case of *free* beauty, — beauty, strictly so called, — both the imagination and the understanding find occupation ; and the pleasure we experience from such an object is in proportion as it affords to these faculties the opportunity of exerting fully and freely their respective energies. Now, it is the principal function of the understanding, out of the multifarious presented to it, to form a whole. Its entire activity is, in fact, a tendency towards unity ; and it is only satisfied when this object is so constituted as to afford the opportunity of an easy and perfect performance of this its function. The object is then judged to be beautiful or pleasing. This enables us to explain the differences of different individuals in the apprehension of the beautiful. If an understanding, by natural constitution, by cultivation and exercise, be vigorous enough to think up rapidly into a whole what is presented in complexity, the individual has an enjoyment, and he regards the object as beautiful ; whereas if an intellect perform this function slowly and with effort, if it succeed in accomplishing the end at all, the individual can feel no pleasure (if he does not experience pain), and the object must to him appear as one destitute of beauty, if not positively ugly. Hence it is that children, boors, in a word persons of a weak or uncultivated mind, may find the parts of a building beautiful, while unable to comprehend the beauty of it as a whole.

(*β*) In the case of *relative* or *dependent* beauty we must distinguish the pleasure we receive into two, combined indeed, but not identical. The one of these pleasures is that from the beauty which the object contains, and the principle of which we have been just considering. The other of these pleasures is that which we showed was attached to a perfect energy of the understanding in thinking an object under the notion of conformity as a mean adapted to an end.

The result, then, of what has now been said is, that *a thing beautiful is one whose form occupies the imagination and understanding in a free and full, and consequently in an agreeable, activity.*

ii. The feeling of pleasure in *the sublime* is essentially different from our feeling of pleasure in the beautiful. The beautiful affords a feeling of unmingled pleasure in the full and unimpeded activity of our cognitive powers; whereas our feeling of sublimity is a mingled one of pleasure and of pain, — of pleasure in the consciousness of strong energy, of pain in the consciousness that this energy is in vain. But as the amount of pleasure in the sublime is greater than the amount of pain, it follows that the free energy it elicits must be greater than the free energy it repels. The beautiful has reference to the form of an object, and the facility with which it is comprehended. For beauty, magnitude is thus an impediment. Sublimity, on the contrary, requires magnitude as its condition; and the formless is not unfrequently sublime. That we are at once attracted and repelled by sublimity, arises from the circumstance that the object, which we call *sublime*, is proportioned to one of our faculties, and disproportioned to another; but as the degree of pleasure transcends the degree of pain, the power whose energy is promoted must be superior to that power whose energy is repressed.

The sublime may be divided, according to the three quantities, into the sublime of extension, the sublime of protension, and the sublime of intension; or, what comes to the same thing, the sublime of space, the sublime of time, and the sublime of power. In the two former the cognitive, in the last the conative, powers come into play.

(*a*) An object is extensively or protensively sublime when it comprises so great a multitude of parts that the imagination sinks under the attempt to represent it in an image, and the understanding to measure it by other quantities. Baffled in the attempt to reduce the object within the limits of the faculties by which it must be comprehended, the mind at once desists from the ineffectual effort, and conceives the object not by a positive, but by a negative, notion; it conceives it as inconceivable, and falls back into repose, which is felt as pleasing by contrast to the continuance of a forced and impeded energy. Examples of the sublime — of this sudden effort, and of this instantaneous desisting from the attempt — are manifested in the extensive sublime of Space, and in the protensive sublime of Eternity.

(*b*) An object is intensively sublime when it involves such a degree of force or power that the imagination cannot at once represent, and the understanding cannot at once bring under measure, the quantum of this force; and when, from the nature of the object, the inability of the mind is at once made apparent, so that it does not proceed in the ineffectual effort, but at once calls back its energies from the attempt.

It is thus manifest that the feeling of the sublime will be one of mingled pain and pleasure; pleasure, from the vigorous exertion and the instantaneous repose; pain, from the consciousness of limited and frustrated activity. This mixed feeling in the contemplation of the sublime object is finely expressed by Lucretius when he says : —

> "Me quædam divina voluptas
> Percipit atque horror."

iii. The *Picturesque*, however opposite to the sublime, seems, in my opinion, to stand to the beautiful in a somewhat similar relation. An object is positively ugly, when it is of such a form that the imagination and the understanding cannot help attempting to think it up into unity, and yet their energies fail in the endeavor, or accomplish it only imperfectly after time and toil. The cause of this continuance of effort is, that the object does not present such an appearance of incongruous variety as at once to compel the mind to desist from the attempt of reducing it to unity; but, on the contrary, leads it on to attempt what it is yet unable to perform, — its reduction to a whole. But variety — variety even apart from unity — is pleasing; and if the mind be made content to expatiate freely and easily in this variety, without attempting painfully to reduce it to unity, it will derive no inconsiderable pleasure from this exertion of its powers. Now, a picturesque object is precisely of such a character. It is so determinately varied and so abrupt in its variety; it presents so complete a negation of all rounded contour, and so regular an irregularity of broken lines and angles; that every attempt at reducing it to an harmonious whole is at once found to be impossible. The mind, therefore, which must forego the energy of representing and thinking the object as a unity, surrenders itself at once to the energies which deal with it only in detail.

II. The *practical* feelings are divisible into five classes, as they relate to (1.) our self-preservation, (2.) the enjoyment of our existence, (3.) the preservation of the species, (4.) our tendency towards development and perfection, (5.) the moral law.

1. The *feelings of self-preservation* are those of hunger and thirst, loathing, sorrow, bodily pain, repose, fear at danger, anxiety, shuddering, alarm, composure, security, and the nameless feeling at the representation of death. Several of these feelings are corporeal, and may be considered, with equal propriety, as modifications of the vague sense.

2. The *feelings relating to the enjoyment of existence* arise from the fact that man is determined not only to exist, but to exist well; he is therefore determined also to desire whatever tends to render life agreeable, and to eschew whatever tends to render it disagreeable. All, therefore, that appears to contribute to the former, causes in him the feeling of joy; whereas

all that seems to threaten the latter excites in him the repressed feelings of fear, anxiety, sorrow, etc., which we have already mentioned.

3. Man is determined not only to preserve himself, but to *preserve the species* to which he belongs, and with this tendency various feelings are associated. To this head belong the feelings of sexual love and parental affection. But the human affections are not limited to family connections. "Man," says Aristotle, " is the sweetest thing to man." We have thus a tendency to social intercourse, and society is at once the necessary condition of our happiness and of our perfection. In conformity with his tendency to social existence man is endowed with a sympathetic feeling; that is, he rejoices with those that rejoice, and grieves with those that grieve. Compassion or pity is the name given to the latter modification of sympathy; the former is without a definite name. Besides sympathetic sorrow and sympathetic joy, there are a variety of feelings which have reference to our existence in a social relation. Of these there is that connected with vanity, or the wish to please others from the desire of being respected by them ; with shame, or the fear and sorrow at incurring their disrespect; with pride, or the overweening sentiment of our own worth. To the same class we may refer the feelings connected with indignation, resentment, anger, scorn, etc.

4. There is in man implanted a desire of developing his powers, — a *tendency towards perfection*. In virtue of this, the consciousness of all comparative inability causes pain; the consciousness of all com-

parative power causes pleasure. To this class belong
the feelings which accompany emulation, — the desire
of rising superior to others ; and envy, — the desire
of reducing others beneath ourselves.

5. We are conscious that there is in man *a moral
law*, which unconditionally commands the fulfilment
of its behests. Inasmuch as moral intelligence unconditionally commands us to perform what we are conscious to be our duty, there is attributed to man an
absolute worth. The feeling, which the manifestation of this worth excites, is called *respect*. With the
consciousness of the lofty nature of our moral tendencies, and our ability to fulfil what the law of duty
prescribes, there is connected the feeling of *self-
respect;* whereas, from a consciousness of the contrast
between what we ought to do and what we actually
perform, there arises the feeling of *self-abasement*.
The sentiment of respect for the law of duty is the
moral feeling, which has by some been improperly
denominated the *moral sense;* for through this feeling
we do not take cognizance whether anything be
morally good or morally evil, but when by our intelligence we recognize aught to be of such a character,
there is herewith associated a feeling of pain or
pleasure, which is nothing more than our state in reference to the fulfilment or violation of the law. Man,
as conscious of his liberty to act and of the law by
which his actions ought to be regulated, recognizes
his personal accountability, and calls himself before
the internal tribunal which we denominate *conscience*.
Here he is either acquitted or condemned. The ac-

quittal is connected with a peculiar feeling of pleasurable exultation, as the condemnation is with a peculiar
feeling of painful humiliation, — remorse.   (*Lect. on
Metaph.*, XLV. and XLVI.)

THIRD PART OF PHENOMENAL PSYCHOLOGY.

PHENOMENOLOGY OF THE CONATIONS.

THIRD PART OF PHENOMENAL PSYCHOLOGY.

PHENOMENOLOGY OF THE CONATIONS.

UNDER the third class of mental phenomena are comprehended both the phenomenon of desire and the phenomenon of volition. In English unfortunately we have no term capable of adequately expressing what is common both to volition and desire, that is, the *nisus* or *conatus*, — the tendency towards the realization of their end. Were we to say the phenomena of *tendency*, the phrase would be vague; and the same is true of the phenomena of *doing*. Again, the term phenomena of *appetency* is objectionable, because .. (to say nothing of the unfamiliarity of the expression) *appetency*, though perhaps etymologically unexceptionable, has, both in Latin and English, a meaning almost synonymous with desire. Like the Latin *appetentia*, the Greek ὄρεξις is equally ill-balanced; for, though used by philosophers to comprehend both will and desire, it more familiarly suggests the latter, and we need not, therefore, be solicitous, with Mr. Harris and Lord Monboddo, to naturalize in English the term *orectic*. Again, the phrase phenomena of *activity* would be even worse; every possible objection

can be made to the term *active powers*, by which the
philosophers of this country have designated the *orectic faculties* of the Aristotelians.   For you will observe that all faculties are equally active; and it is
not the overt performance, but the tendency towards
it, for which we are in quest of an expression.   The
term *Conative* is employed by Cudworth, and I shall
adopt the word *conations* as the most appropriate
expression for this class of phenomena.   (*Lect. on
Metaph.*, XI.)

The conations, as tendencies to action, are divisible
into classes, as such tendencies are either blind and
fatal, or deliberate and free.   The former are *desires*,
the latter, *volitions*.

(A) DESIRES may be subdivided according to their
objects, for they relate either (1.) to Self-preservation, or (2.) to the Enjoyment of Existence, or (3.)
to the Preservation of the Species, or (4.) to our
Tendency towards Development and Perfection, or
(5.) to the Moral Law.[1]   (*Lect. on Metaph.*, XLVI.)

II.   WILL is a free cause, a cause which is not also
an effect, a power of absolute origination.   (*Discussions*, p. 623.)   It is proved to be so,

1. *Directly*, by an immediate testimony of consciousness to the fact (*Lect. on Metaph.*, II.; *Reid's
Works*, p. 624, note, and pp. 616–7, notes); while

---

[1] It may be observed that this is the classification of the desires
given above (*Phenomenology of the Feelings*, Chap. II., § 2, (B)
II.); and it is the only classification attempted by Sir William Hamilton.   It ought not, however, to be forgotten that it is suggested,
not in an independent treatment of the desires, but in a description
of the feelings which the desires originate. — J. C. M.

2. *Indirectly* also it is implied in our consciousness, at once of an uncompromising law of duty, and of our being the accountable authors of our actions. (*Lect. on Metaph.*, II. ; *Discussions*, pp. 623–4.)

The fact of a free volition is indeed positively inconceivable, and that for two reasons : —

1. The Law of the *Conditioned in Time*, under the form of the Law of Causality, renders impossible the conception of an absolute commencement.

2. On the one hand, the determination of the will by motives can be conceived only as a necessitation which would render moral accountability impossible. On the other hand, were we to admit as true what we cannot think as possible, still the doctrine of a motiveless volition would be only casualism ; and the free acts of an indifferent, are, morally and rationally, as worthless as the pre-ordered passions of a determined will.

How, therefore, moral liberty is possible in man or in God must remain, under the present limitation of our faculties, wholly incomprehensible ; but the *fact* of liberty cannot be redargued on the ground of its incomprehensibility. For,

1. The judgment of causality, which renders free will inconceivable, has been proved not to depend on a *power* of the mind, imposing, as necessary in thought, what is necessary in the universe of existence. This judgment is a mere mental *impotence*, — an impotence to conceive either of two contradictories ; and as the *one* or the *other* of contradictories must be true, whilst both cannot, there is no ground for inferring a fact to be impossible merely from *our inability to conceive its*

possibility. At the same time, if the causal judgment be not an express affirmation of mind, but only an incapacity of thinking the opposite, it follows that such a negative judgment cannot counterbalance the express affirmative, the unconditional testimony, of consciousness, that we are, though we know not how, the true and responsible authors of our actions, not merely the worthless links in an adamantine series of causes and effects.

2. But not only may the fact of our moral liberty be shown to be possible, though inconceivable; the very objection of incomprehensibility, by which the fatalist had thought to triumph over the libertarian, may be retorted against himself. The scheme of freedom is not more inconceivable than the scheme of necessity. For whilst fatalism is a recoil from the more obtrusive inconceivability of an *absolute* commencement, on the fact of which commencement the doctrine of liberty proceeds; the fatalist overlooks the equal, but less obtrusive, inconceivability of an *infinite* non-commencement, on the assertion of which non-commencement his own doctrine of necessity must ultimately rest. As equally unthinkable, the two counter, the two one-sided, schemes are thus theoretically balanced. But practically our consciousness of the moral law, which, without a moral liberty in man, would be a mendacious imperative, gives a decisive preponderance to the doctrine of freedom over the doctrine of fate. We are free in act, if we are accountable for our actions. (*Discussions*, pp. 623–5.)

SECOND DIVISION OF PHILOSOPHY.

NOMOLOGICAL PSYCHOLOGY.

NOMOLOGICAL PSYCHOLOGY.

NOMOLOGICAL PSYCHOLOGY, or the Nomology of
Mind, is that science which investigates, not contingent appearances, but the *necessary* and *universal*
facts, that is, the *laws*, by which our faculties are
governed, to the end that we may obtain a criterion
by which to judge or to explain their procedures and
manifestations. Now, there will be as many depart-
ments of Nomological Psychology as there are classes
of mental phenomena; for as each class proposes a
different end, and, in the accomplishment of that end,
is regulated by peculiar laws, each must consequently
have a different science conversant about these laws,
that is, a different Nomology.

(A) FIRST PART OF NOMOLOGICAL PSYCHOLOGY:
NOMOLOGY OF THE COGNITIONS. There is no one, no
Nomological, science of the Cognitive faculties, in
general; though we have some older treatises which,
though partial in their subject, afford a name not un-
suitable for a nomology of the cognitions, — namely,
Gnoseologia or Gnostologia. There is no independent science of the laws of Perception; if there were,
it might be called Æsthetic, which, however, as we
shall see, would be ambiguous. Mnemonic, or the

231

science of the laws of Memory, has been elaborated
at least in numerous treatises; but the name Anam-
nestic, the art of Recollection or Reminiscence, might
be equally well applied to it.   The laws of the Representative faculty, — that is, the laws of Association, —
have not yet been elevated into a separate Nomological science.   Neither have the conditions of the Regulative or Legislative faculty, the faculty itself of
Laws, been fully analyzed, far less reduced to system;
though we have several deservedly forgotten treatises,
of an older date, under the inviting name of *Noölo-
gies.*   The only one of the cognitive faculties, whose
laws constitute the object-matter of a separate science,
is the Elaborative.   This Nomology has obtained the
name of Logic [1] among other appellations, but not
from Aristotle.   The best name would have been
Dianoetic.   Logic is the science of the laws of
thought in relation to the end which our cognitive
faculties propose, — *i. e.*, the True.   To this head
might be referred Grammar, — Universal Grammar,
Philosophical Grammar, or the science conversant
with the laws of Language, as the instrument of
thought.

(B) Second Part of Nomological Psychology :
Nomology of the Feelings.   The Nomology of our
Feelings, or the science of the laws which govern our
capacities of enjoyment, in relation to the end which
they propose, — *i. e.*, the Pleasurable, — has obtained no precise name in our language.   It has been

---

[1] Sir William Hamilton has a separate course of lectures on Logic,
which, however, could not, even in the most abridged form, be em-
bodied in the present work. — J. C. M.

called the Philosophy of Taste, and, on the Continent especially, it has been denominated Æsthetic. Neither name is unobjectionable. The first is vague, metaphorical, and even delusive. In regard to the second, you are aware that αἴσθησις in Greek means feeling in general, as well as sense in particular; as our term *feeling* means either the sense of touch in particular, or sentiment, — and the capacity of the pleasurable and painful in general. Both terms are, therefore, to a certain extent, ambiguous; but this objection can rarely be avoided, and Æsthetic, if not the best expression to be found, has already been long and generally employed. The term Apolaustic would have been a more appropriate designation.

(C) THIRD PART OF NOMOLOGICAL PSYCHOLOGY: NOMOLOGY OF THE CONATIONS. The Nomology of our Conative powers is *Practical Philosophy*, properly so called; for practical philosophy is simply the science of the laws regulative of our will and desires in relation to the end which our conative powers propose, — *i. e.*, the GOOD. This, as it considers these laws in relation to man as an individual, or in relation to man as a member of society, will be divided into two branches, — Ethics and Politics; and these again admit of various subdivisions. (*Lect. on Metaph.*, VII.)

THIRD DIVISION OF PHILOSOPHY.

INFERENTIAL PSYCHOLOGY.

CHAPTER I.

EXISTENCE IN GENERAL.

In connection with the general division of the phil osophical sciences it was stated that the third great branch of philosophy investigates the inferences which are to be drawn from the phenomena presented in consciousness. It is not, therefore, to be supposed that we have an immediate knowledge of existence itself; we know it merely through the phenomena in which it is manifested. It is consequently necessary now to explain the great axiom, that *all human knowledge is only of the relative and phenomenal.*

In this proposition the term *relative* is opposed to the term *absolute;* and therefore, in saying that we know only the relative, I virtually assert that we know nothing absolute, — nothing existing absolutely, that is, in and for itself, and without relation to us and our faculties. I shall illustrate this by its application. Our knowledge is either of *matter* or of *mind.*

I. Now, what is *matter?* What do we know of

matter? Matter or body is to us the name either of something *known* or of something *unknown*.

1. In so far as matter is the name for *something known*, it means that which appears to us under the forms of extension, solidity, divisibility, figure, motion, roughness, smoothness, color, heat, cold, etc. ; in short, it is a common name for a certain series or aggregate or complement of appearances or phenomena manifested in coexistence.

2. But as these phenomena appear only in conjunction, we are compelled by the constitution of our nature to think them conjoined in and by something ; and as they are phenomena, we cannot think them the phenomena of nothing, but must regard them as the properties or qualities of something that is extended, solid, figured, etc. But this something, absolutely and in itself, — that is, considered apart from its phenomena, — is to us as zero. It is only in its qualities, only in its effects, in its relative or phenomenal existence, that it is cognizable or conceivable ; and it is only by a law of thought, which compels us to think something, absolute and unknown, as the basis or condition of the relative and known, that this something obtains a kind of incomprehensible reality to us. Now, that which manifests its qualities, — in other words, that in which the appearing causes inhere, that to which they belong, — is called their *subject*, or *substance*, or *substratum*. To this subject of the phenomena of extension, solidity, etc., the term *matter* or *material substance* is commonly given ; and, therefore, as contradistinguished from these qualities, it is the name of *something unknown* and inconceivable.

II. The same is true in regard to the term *mind.*
1. In so far as mind is the common name for the
states of knowing, willing, feeling, desiring, etc., of
which I am conscious, it is only the name for a certain
series of connected phenomena or qualities, and, consequently, expresses only what is *known.* 2. But in
so far as it denotes that subject or substance in which
the phenomena of knowing, willing, etc., inhere, —
something behind or under these phenomena, — it
expresses what, in itself, or in its absolute existence,
is *unknown.*

Thus, mind and matter, as known or knowable, are
only two different series of phenomena or qualities;
mind and matter, as unknown and unknowable, are
the two substances in which these two different series
of phenomena or qualities are supposed to inhere.
The existence of an unknown substance is only an inference we are compelled to make from the existence
of known phenomena; and the distinction of two
substances is only inferred from the seeming incom-
patibility of the two series of phenomena to coinhere
in one.

Our whole knowledge of mind and matter is thus,
as we have said, only relative; of existence, absolutely and in itself, we know nothing; and we may
say of man what Virgil says of Æneas, contemplating
in the prophetic sculpture of his shield the future
glories of Rome, —

" Rerumque ignarus, imagine gaudet."

Thus, our knowledge is of partial and relative existence only, seeing that existence in itself, or abso-

lute existence, is no object of knowledge. But it does not follow that all relative existence is relative to *us;* that all that can be known even by a limited intelligence is actually cognizable by us. We must, therefore, more precisely limit our sphere of knowledge, by adding, that all we know is known only under the special conditions of knowledge.

Now, this principle of the relativity of all human knowledge divides itself into two branches. In the *first* place, it would be unphilosophical to conclude that the properties of existence necessarily are, *in number*, only as the number of our faculties of appre hending them ; or, in the *second*, that the properties known are known *in their native purity*, and without addition or modification from our organs of sense, or our capacities of intelligence. I shall illustrate these in their order.

I. In regard to the first assertion, it is evident that nothing exists for us, except in so far as it is known to us, and that nothing is known to us, except certain properties or modes of existence, which are relative or analogous to our faculties. Beyond these modes we know, and can assert, the reality of no existence. But if, on the one hand, we are not entitled to assert, as actually existent, except what we know ; neither, on the other, are we warranted in denying, as possibly existent, what we do not know. The universe may be conceived as a polygon of a thousand, or a hundred thousand, sides or facets ; and each of these sides or facets may be conceived as representing one special mode of existence. Now, of these thousand sides or modes, all may be equally essential, but three

or four only may be turned towards us, or be analogous to our organs. One side or facet of the universe, as holding a relation to the organ of sight, is
the mode of luminous or visible existence; another,
as proportional to the organ of hearing, is the mode
of sonorous or audible existence; and so on. But if
every eye to see, if every ear to hear, were annihilated, the mode of existence to which these organs
now stand in relation, — that which could be seen,
that which could be heard, — would still remain; and
if the intelligences, reduced to the three senses of
touch, smell, and taste, were then to assert the impossibility of any modes of being except those to
which these three senses were analogous, the procedure
would not be more unwarranted, than if we now ventured to deny the possible reality of other modes of
material existence than those to the perception of
which our five senses are accommodated. I will illustrate this by a hypothetical parallel. Let us suppose
a block of marble, on which there are four different
inscriptions, — in Greek, in Latin, in Persic, in He-
brew; and that four travellers approach, each able to
read only the inscription in his native tongue. The
Greek is delighted with the information the marble
affords him of the siege of Troy; the Roman finds
interesting matter regarding the expulsion of the
Kings; the Persian deciphers an oracle of Zoroaster,
and the Jew is surprised by a commemoration of the
Exodus. Here, as each inscription exists or is significant only to him who possesses the corresponding
language; so the several modes of existence are manifested only to those intelligences who possess the

16

corresponding organs. And as each of the four
readers would be rash, if he maintained that the marble could be significant only as significant to him, so
should we be rash, were we to hold that the universe
had no other phases of being than the few that are
turned towards our faculties, and which our five senses
enable us to perceive.

Before leaving this subject, it is perhaps proper to
observe that, had we faculties equal in number to all
the possible modes of existence, whether of mind or
matter, still would our knowledge of mind or matter
be only relative. If material existence could exhibit
ten thousand phenomena, and if we possessed ten
thousand senses to apprehend these, of existence absolutely and in itself we should be then as ignorant as
we are at present.

II. But the consideration that our actual faculties
of knowledge are probably wholly inadequate in number to the possible modes of being, is of comparatively
less importance than the other consideration to which
we now proceed, that whatever we know is *not known
as it is, but only as it seems to us to be;* for it is of
less importance that our knowledge should be limited,
than that our knowledge should be pure. It is, therefore, of the highest moment that we should be aware
that what we know is not a simple relation apprehended between the object known and the subject
knowing, but that every knowledge is a sum made up
of several elements, and that the great business of
philosophy is to analyze and discriminate these elements, and to determine from whence these contribu-
tions have been derived. I shall explain what I mean

by an example. In the perception of an external
object, the mind does not know it in immediate relation to itself, but mediately, in relation to the material organs of sense. If, therefore, we were to throw
these organs out of consideration, and did not take
into account what they contribute to, and how they
modify our knowledge of, that object, it is evident
that our conclusion in regard to the nature of external
perception would be erroneous. Again, an object of
perception may not even stand in immediate relation
to the organ of sense, but may make its impression on
that organ through an intervening medium. Now, if
this medium be thrown out of account, and if it be
not considered that the real external object is the sum
of all that externally contributes to affect the sense,
we shall, in like manner, run into error. For example, I see a book, — I see that book through an external medium (what that medium is, we do not now
inquire), — and I see it through my organ of sight,
the eye. Now, as the full object presented to the
mind (observe that I say *the mind*), in perception, is
an object compounded of (1.) the external object
emitting or reflecting light, *i. e.*, modifying the external medium, of (2.) this external medium, and of (3.)
the living organ of sense, in their mutual relation, let
us suppose, in the example I have taken, that the full
or adequate object perceived is equal to twelve, and
that this amount is made up of three several parts, —
of four contributed by the book, of four contributed
by all that intervenes between the book and the
organ, and of four contributed by the living organ
itself.

I use this illustration to show, that the phenomenon of the 'external object is not presented immediately to the mind, but is known by it only as
modified through certain intermediate agencies; and
to show that sense itself may be a source of error, if
we do not analyze and distinguish what elements, in
an act of perception, belong to the outward reality,
what to the outward medium, and what to the action
of sense itself.   But this source of error is not limited
to our perceptions; and we are liable to be deceived,
not merely by not distinguishing in an act of knowledge what is contributed by sense, but by not distinguishing what is contributed by the mind itself.
This is the most difficult and important function of
philosophy; and the greater number of its higher
problems arise in the attempt to determine the shares
to which the knowing subject, and the object known,
may pretend in the total act of cognition. For, according as we attribute a larger or a smaller proportion to
each, we either run into the extremes of Idealism and
Materialism, or maintain an equilibrium between the
two.   (*Lect. on Metaph.*, VIII.)

But although existence be only revealed to us in
phenomena, and though we can, therefore, have only
a relative knowledge either of mind or of matter; still,
by inference and analogy, we may legitimately attempt
to rise above the mere appearances which experience
and observation afford.   Thus, for example, the existence of God and the Immortality of the Soul are
not given us as phenomena, as objects of immediate
knowledge; yet, if the phenomena actually given do

necessarily require, for their rational explanation, the hypotheses of immortality and of God, we are assuredly entitled, from the existence of the former, to infer the reality of the latter.   (*Ibid.*, VII.)

CHAPTER II.

EXISTENCE OF GOD AND IMMORTALITY OF THE SOUL.

THE mind of man rises to its highest dignity when viewed as the object through which, and through which alone, his unassisted reason can ascend to the knowledge of a God.

The Deity is not an object of immediate contemplation; as existing and in himself, he is beyond our reach; we can know him only mediately through his works, and are only warranted in assuming his existence as a certain kind of cause necessary to account for a certain state of things, of whose reality our faculties are supposed to inform us. The affirmation of a God being thus a regressive inference, from the existence of a special class of effects to the existence of a special character of cause, it is evident that the whole argument hinges on the fact, — Does a state of things really exist such as is only possible through the agency of a Divine Cause? For if it can be shown that such a state of things does not really exist, then

246

our inference to the kind of cause requisite to account
for it is necessarily null.

We must, first of all, then, consider what kind of
cause it is which constitutes a Deity, and what kind
of effects they are which allow us to infer that a Deity
must be.

The notion of a God is not contained in the notion
of a mere first cause ; for in the admission of a first
cause Atheist and Theist are at one. Neither is this
notion completed by adding to a first cause the attribute of Omnipotence ; for the atheist who holds matter or necessity to be the original principle of all that
is, does not convert his blind force into a God, by
merely affirming it to be all-powerful. It is not until
the two great attributes of Intelligence and Virtue
(and be it observed that Virtue involves Liberty) — I
say, it is not until the two attributes of intelligence
and virtue or holiness are brought in, that the belief
in a primary and omnipotent cause becomes the belief in a veritable Divinity. But these latter attributes are not more essential to the divine nature than
are the former. For as original and infinite power
does not of itself constitute a God, so neither is a God
constituted by intelligence and virtue, unless intelligence and goodness be themselves conjoined with this
original and infinite power. For even a Creator,
intelligent and good and powerful, would be no God,
were he dependent for his intelligence and goodness
and power on any higher principle. On this supposition, the perfections of the Creator are viewed as limited and derived. He is himself, therefore, only a
dependency, — only a creature ; and if a God there

be, he must be sought for in that higher principle, from which this subordinate principle derives its attributes. Now, is this highest principle (*ex hypothese,* all-powerful) also intelligent and moral; then it is itself the veritable Deity. On the other hand, is it, though the author of intelligence and goodness in another, itself unintelligent; then is a blind Fate constituted the first and universal cause, and atheism is asserted.

The peculiar attributes which distinguish a Deity from the original omnipotence or blind fate of the atheist being thus those of intelligence and holiness of will, and the assertion of theism being only the assertion that the universe is governed not only by physical but by moral laws, we have next to consider how we are warranted in these two affirmations : (1.) that intelligence stands first in the absolute order of existence, in other words, that final preceded efficient causes ; and (2.) that the universe is governed by moral laws.

The proof of these two propositions is the proof of a God ; but before considering how far the phenomena of mind and of matter do and do not allow us to infer the one position or the other, I must solicit your attention to the characteristic contrasts which these two classes of phenomena in themselves exhibit.

In the compass of our experience, we distinguish two series of facts, — the facts of the external or material world, and the facts of the internal world or world of intelligence. These concomitant series of phenomena are not like streams which merely run parallel to each other ; they do not, like the Alpheus and Arethusa, flow on side by side without a commingling of their waters. They cross, they combine, they are interlaced; but notwithstanding their intimate connection, their mutual action and reaction, we are able to discriminate them without difficulty, because they are marked out by characteristic differences.

The phenomena of the material world are subjected to immutable laws, are produced and reproduced in the same invariable succession, and manifest only the blind force of a mechanical necessity.

The phenomena of man are, in part, subjected to the laws of the external universe. As dependent upon a bodily organization, as actuated by sensual propensities and animal wants, he belongs to matter, and, in this respect, he is the slave of necessity. But what man holds of matter does not make up his personality. They are his, not he; man is not an organism, — he is an intelligence served by organs. For in man there are tendencies — there is a law — which continually urge him to prove that he is more powerful than the nature by which he is surrounded and penetrated. He is conscious to himself of faculties not comprised in the chain of physical necessity; his intelligence reveals prescriptive principles of action, absolute and universal, in the Law of Duty, and a liberty capable of carrying that law into effect, in opposition to the solicitations, the impulsions, of his material nature. From the coexistence of these opposing forces in man, there results a ceaseless struggle between physical necessity and moral liberty, — in the language of Revelation, between the Flesh and the Spirit; and this

struggle constitutes at once the distinctive character
of humanity, and the essential condition of human
development and virtue.

In the facts of intelligence we thus become aware
of an order of things diametrically in contrast to that
displayed to us in the facts of the material universe.
There is made known to us an order of things, in
which intelligence, by recognizing the unconditional
law of duty and an absolute obligation to fulfil it, recognizes its own possession of a liberty incompatible
with a dependence upon fate, and of a power capable
of resisting and conquering the counteraction of our
animal nature.

Now, it is only as man is a free intelligence, a
moral power, that he is created after the image of
God, and it is only as a spark of divinity glows as the
life of life in us, that we can rationally believe in an
Intelligent Creator and Moral Governor of the universe. For, let us suppose that in man intelligence
is the product of organization, that our consciousness
of moral liberty is itself an illusion; in short, that
acts of volition are results of the same iron necessity
which determines the phenomena of matter; on this
supposition the foundations of all religion, natural and
revealed, are subverted. The truth of this will be
best seen by applying the supposition of the two positions of theism previously stated.

I. In regard to the former, how can we attempt to
prove that *the universe is the creation of a free original
intelligence*, against the counterposition of the atheist,
that liberty is an illusion, and intelligence, or the
adaptation of means to ends, only the product of a

blind fate? As we know nothing of the absolute order of existence in itself, we can only attempt to infer its character from that of the particular order within the sphere of our experience; and as we can affirm naught of intelligence and its conditions except what we may discover from the observation of our own minds, it is evident that we can only analogically carry out into the order of the universe the relation in which we find intelligence to stand in the order of the human constitution. If in man intelligence be a free power, in so far as its liberty extends, intelligence must be independent of necessity and matter; and a power independent of matter necessarily implies the existence of an immaterial subject, that is, a spirit. If, then, the original independence of intelligence on matter in the human constitution, in other words, if the spirituality of mind in man, be supposed a datum of observation, in this datum is also given both the condition and the proof of a God. For we have only to infer, what analogy entitles us to do, that intelligence holds the same relative supremacy in the universe which it holds in us, and the first positive condition of a Deity is established, in the establishment of the absolute priority of a free creative intelligence. On the other hand, let us suppose the result of our study of man to be, that intelligence is only a product of matter, only a reflex of organization, such a doctrine would not only afford no basis on which to rest any argument for a God, but, on the contrary, would positively warrant the atheist in denying his existence. For if, as the materialist maintains, the only intelligence of which we have any experience be a consequent of matter, — on this hypothesis, he not only cannot assume this order to be reversed in the relations of an intelligence beyond his observation, but, if he argue logically, he must positively conclude, that, as in man, so in the universe, the phenomena of intelligence or design are only in their last analysis the products of a brute necessity. Psychological materialism, if carried out fully and fairly to its conclusions, thus inevitably results in theological atheism; as it has been well expressed by Dr. Henry More, *nullus in microcosmo spiritus, nullus in macrocosmo Deus.* I do not, of course, mean to assert that all materialists deny, or actually disbelieve, a God. For, in very many cases, this would be at once an unmerited compliment to their reasoning, and an unmerited reproach to their faith.

II. Such is the manifest dependence of our theology on our psychology in reference to the first condition of a Deity, — the absolute priority of a free intelligence. But this is perhaps even more conspicuous in relation to the second, *that the universe is governed not merely by physical but by moral laws;* for God is only God inasmuch as he is the Moral Governor of a Moral World.

Our interest, also, in its establishment is incomparably greater; for while a proof that the universe is the work of an omnipotent intelligence gratifies only our speculative curiosity, — a proof that there is a holy legislator, by whom goodness and felicity will be ultimately brought into accordance, is necessary to satisfy both our intellect and our heart. A God is, indeed, to us, only of practical interest, inasmuch as he is the condition of our immortality.

Now, it is self-evident, in the first place, that, if there be no moral world, there can be no moral governor of such a world; and, in the second, .that we have, and can have, no ground on which to believe in the reality of a moral world, except in so far as we ourselves are moral agents. This being undeniable, it is further evident, that, should we ever be convinced that we are not moral agents, we should likewise be convinced that there exists no moral order in the universe, and no supreme intelligence by which that moral order is established, sustained, and regulated.

But in what does the character of man as a moral agent consist? Man is a moral agent only as he is accountable for his actions, in other words, as he is the object of praise or blame; and this he is only inasmuch as he has prescribed to him a rule of duty, and as he is able to act, or not to act, in conformity with its precepts. The possibility of morality thus depends on the possibility of liberty; for if man be not a free agent, he is not the author of his actions, and has therefore no responsibility, no moral personality, at all.

Theology is thus wholly dependent on psychology or mental science; and psychology operates in three ways to establish that assurance of human liberty which is necessary for a rational belief in our own moral nature, in a moral world, and in a moral ruler of that world.

1. In the first place, an attentive consideration of

the phenomena of mind is necessary in order to a luminous and distinct apprehension of liberty as a datum of intelligence.

2. In the second place, a profound philosophy is necessary to obviate the difficulties which meet us when we attempt to explain the possibility of this fact, and to prove that the datum of liberty is not a mere illusion. For, though an unconquerable feeling compels us to recognize ourselves as accountable, and therefore free agents, still, when we attempt to realize in thought how the fact of our liberty can be, we soon find that this altogether transcends our understanding, and that every effort to bring the fact of liberty within the compass of our conceptions only results in the substitution in its place of some more or less disguised form of necessity. The tendency of a superficial philosophy is therefore to deny the fact of liberty, on the principle that what cannot be conceived is impossible. A deeper and more comprehensive study of the facts of mind overturns this conclusion and destroys its foundation. It proves to us, from the very laws of mind, that, while we can never understand *how* any original datum of intelligence is possible, we have no reason from this inability to doubt that it is true.

3. In the third place, the study of mind is necessary to counterbalance and correct the influence of the study of matter; and this utility of psychology rises in proportion to the progress of the natural sciences, and to the greater attention which they engross. An exclusive devotion to physical pursuits exerts an evil influence in two ways. In the *first* place, it di-

verts from all notice of the phenomena of moral liberty, which are revealed to us in the recesses of the
human mind alone ; and it disqualifies from appreciat-
ing the import of these phenomena, even if presented,
by leaving uncultivated the finer power of psychological reflection, in the exclusive exercise of the faculties
employed in the easier and more amusing observation
of the external world. In the *second* place, by exhib-
iting merely the phenomena of matter and extension,
it habituates us only to the contemplation of an order
in which everything is determined by the laws of a
blind or mechanical necessity. Now, what is the
inevitable tendency of this one-sided and exclusive
study? That the student becomes a materialist, if he
speculate at all. For, in the first place, he is familiar
with the obtrusive facts of necessity, and is unaccus-
tomed to develop into consciousness the more recon-
dite facts of liberty; he is, therefore, disposed to
disbelieve in the existence of phenomena whose reality
he may deny, and whose possibility he cannot understand. At the same time, the love of unity, and the
philosophical presumption against the multiplication
of essences determine him to reject the assumption
of a second, and that an hypothetical, substance, ignorant as he is of the reasons by which that assumption is legitimated.

In the infancy of science, this tendency of physical
study was not experienced. When men first turned
their attention on the phenomena of nature, every
event was viewed as a miracle, for every effect was
considered as the operation of an intelligence. God
was not exiled from the universe of matter; on the

contrary, he was multiplied in proportion to its phenomena. As science advanced, the deities were gradually driven out; and long after the sublunary world had been disenchanted, they were left for a season in possession of the starry heavens. The movement of the celestial bodies, in which Kepler still saw the agency of a free intelligence, was at length by Newton resolved into a few mathematical principles; and at last, even the irregularities which Newton was compelled to leave for the miraculous correction of the Deity, have been proved to require no supernatural interposition; for La Place has shown that all contingencies, past and future, in the heavens, find their explanation in the one fundamental law of gravitation.

But the very contemplation of an order and adaptation so astonishing, joined to the knowledge that this order and adaptation are the necessary results of a brute mechanism, when acting upon minds which have not looked into themselves for the light of which the world without can only afford them reflection, far from elevating them more than any other aspect of external creation to that inscrutable Being who reigns beyond and above the universe of nature, tends, on the contrary, to impress on them, with peculiar force, the conviction, that as the mechanism of nature can explain so much, the mechanism of nature can explain all.

Should physiology ever succeed in reducing the facts of intelligence to phenomena of matter, philosophy would be subverted in the subversion of its three great objects, GOD, FREE-WILL, and IMMORTALITY.

True wisdom would then consist, not in speculation, but in repressing thought during our brief transit from nothingness to nothingness. For why? Philosophy would have become a meditation, not merely of death, but of annihilation; the precept, *Know thyself*, would have been replaced by the terrible oracle to Œdipus : —

"May'st thou never know the truth of what thou art;"

and the final recompense of our scientific curiosity would be wailing, deeper than Cassandra's, for the ignorance that saved us from despair. (*Lect. on Metaph.*, II.)

www.ingramcontent.com/pod-product-compliance
Lightning Source LLC
Chambersburg PA
CBHW031405020726
47499CB00005B/1476